For Mum, Mo, Dad, Ann, Emma, James, Alice and Evie.
You are my backbone and my joy.

Tom Stuart

AFTER EDWARD

OBERON BOOKS
LONDON

WWW.OBERONBOOKS.COM

First published in 2019 by Oberon Books Ltd
521 Caledonian Road, London N7 9RH
Tel: +44 (0) 20 7607 3637 / Fax: +44 (0) 20 7607 3629
e-mail: info@oberonbooks.com
www.oberonbooks.com

A catalogue record for this book is available from the British Library.

PB ISBN: 9781786827050
E ISBN: 9781786827067

Cover image: Premm Design

eBook conversion by Lapiz Digital Services, India.

Visit www.oberonbooks.com to read more about all our books and to buy them. You will also find features, author interviews and news of any author events, and you can sign up for e-newsletters so that you're always first to hear about our new releases.

10 9 8 7 6 5 4 3 2 1

Acknowledgements

Thanks to early readers and encouragers:
Katie McGuiness, Jack Laskey, Ellen McDougall,
Nick Bagnall and Caroline Steinbeiss.

For research I read a lot of books and spoke to some
brilliant people, including Philippa Perry, Nick Kientsch,
Stephen Daly and the wonderful Dr Will Tosh – thank you.

This production has been blessed with an exceptional
cast and team. Without their support, talent, friendship
and dedication these words would be private thoughts
inhabiting a silent page.

Thank you Brendan O'Hea for your patience,
your wit, your heart.

And finally, thanks to Shakespeare's Globe
and to the tenacious, mighty Michelle Terry.

The Globe is an organisation so fuelled by love, kindness
and care that its very structures defy their definitions –
it is less a building, more a mensch.

After Edward was first performed at the Sam Wanamaker Playhouse, London on 21 March 2019. Cast and creatives were as follows:

Cast

Annette Badland	GERTRUDE STEIN
Brian Bartle /	ERROL
Seyi Andes-Pelumi	
Richard Bremmer	ARCHBISHOP OF CANTERBURY/ LEATHER MAN
Richard Cant	QUENTIN CRISP
Polly Frame	HARVEY MILK
Jonathan Livingstone	EDWARD ALLEYN
Sanchia McCormack	MARGARET THATCHER
Colin Ryan	COWBOY
Tom Stuart	EDWARD
Beru Tessema	GAVESTON
Katie West	DOROTHY GALE/ MARIA VON TRAPP

Creatives

Sarah Case	Voice
Glynn MacDonald	Globe Associate – Movement
Laura Moody	Composer
George Nichols	Assistant Director
Brendan O'Hea	Director
Jan Haydn Rowles	Dialect Coach
Siân Williams	Choreographer
Jessica Worrall	Designer

A few notes.

The structure and decor of the theatre should remain as is.

All entrances should be fitted with doors.
All doors should have the appearance of being able
to open and close of their own accord.

The action takes place over one act, without an interval.

EDWARD manages to sit up, rubs his head, takes in his surroundings.

What is this?

CANTERBURY: What is what?

EDWARD: This.

CANTERBURY: *(The candelabra.) This?*

EDWARD: No this. *(The space.)* Where am I?

CANTERBURY: Here.

EDWARD: Yes but where is here?

CANTERBURY: It's *here*, isn't it… I'm sorry, I don't think I'm following –

EDWARD: Did something happen?

CANTERBURY: Yes, you fell. We've covered that. Didn't bend your knees, remember?

EDWARD: Before that, before I fell…

CANTERBURY chuckles to himself.

CANTERBURY: All sorts went on.

EDWARD looks at him expectantly. CANTERBURY is oblivious, focused on his candle duties.

EDWARD: You were saying?

CANTERBURY: Was I?

EDWARD: What happened –

CANTERBURY: Terrible pickle.

EDWARD: Okay.

CANTERBURY: Positively grizzly it was in the end.

EDWARD: What was?

CANTERBURY: Listen, should you be sitting up? I imagine you must be smarting. That's a hardwood floor that. Oak by the looks of it –

EDWARD: Am I dead?

CANTERBURY: Do what now?

EDWARD: Dead. Am I dead?

CANTERBURY: I shouldn't think so.

EDWARD: Okay.

Beat.

CANTERBURY: You look disappointed.

EDWARD: I was expecting more of a definitive answer. I thought you'd be more of an authority.

CANTERBURY: On what?

EDWARD: Death… Dressed like that.

CANTERBURY: I get that a lot. I'm quite taken with it, between us. I was ambivalent about the skirt at first, but I like the way it swishes round a corner – it adds an unexpected flourish to almost any entrance.

EDWARD: … Have we met?

CANTERBURY: What's that?

EDWARD: Have we met?

CANTERBURY: When?

EDWARD: Before now? Have we met?

CANTERBURY: Oh, that's a blow.

CANTERBURY stops lighting the candles.

He takes off his hat, shakes his head and sighs.

He collects himself.

But you know what? You've had a fall. I'm gonna put it down to that and move on.

He puts his hat back on and resumes lighting the candles.

EDWARD: Sorry I didn't mean to –

CANTERBURY: Please. Not another word about it.

He begins lighting a particularly tricky, hard to reach candle.

There's a knack to this. Not as easy as it looks. You need a steady hand.

EDWARD: You're doing a great job.

CANTERBURY: That's good of you.

EDWARD: It looks lovely.

CANTERBURY: Doesn't it?

He stands back and admires his work.

Of course, your problem is you're not worthy of love –

He looks at EDWARD, alarmed.

What's that?

EDWARD: Sorry?

CANTERBURY: I thought you said something.

EDWARD: I didn't say anything.

CANTERBURY: Forgive me I thought you did.

EDWARD: It was you, you said something about love –

CANTERBURY: *(Chuckling.)* Love? I don't believe I did. I'm not the sort. Must've been the wind.

He licks his finger and holds it in the air.

There's a definite draft in here. They deny it, but there is. Plays havoc with this lot *(The candles.)* I can tell you.

EDWARD: *(Remembering.)* ... Canterbury.

CANTERBURY: Do what?

EDWARD: You're Canterbury.

CANTERBURY smiles at him.

He finishes lighting a candelabra, admires it.

CANTERBURY: Sometimes it's the little things that just trip my heart into joy.

He gives the candelabra a little spin.

Lovely jubbly.

His demeanour suddenly changes, he becomes formal. His voice resonant, refined and strong. As though possessed by something, he looks out into the distance –

You shall not lie with a male as with a woman; it is an abomination.

EDWARD: Pardon?

CANTERBURY: If a man lies with a male as with a woman, both of them have committed an abomination; they shall surely be put to death; their blood is upon them.

EDWARD is baffled, he stands, looks around trying to see who CANTERBURY is talking to.

Or do you not know that the unrighteous will not inherit the kingdom of God? Do not be deceived: neither the sexually immoral, nor idolaters, nor adulterers, nor men who practice homosexuality, nor thieves, nor the greedy, nor drunkards, nor revilers, nor swindlers will inherit the kingdom of God.

CANTERBURY snaps back to his casual demeanour, rubs his hands together –

Well if that's everything?

EDWARD Sorry?

CANTERBURY: I said if that's everything. It's a figure of speech. I'm off. I'd stick around but I've got mates in. Quick pint then a cycle home I think.

He surveys the lit candles.

Yep, they're all lit. That should give you just about enough I think.

EDWARD: Enough what?

CANTERBURY: Light.

EDWARD: Then what?

CANTERBURY: Well, darkness.

He exits.

Beat.

EDWARD looks around uncertainly.

He looks up at the ceiling. The hatch he fell through is now shut, he can't understand where he fell from.

He rubs his head.

He attempts to follow CANTERBURY out through the same doors.

The doors are now locked. He struggles with them, they won't budge.

He tries the stage right door – it's locked.

He tries the stage left door – it's also locked.

EDWARD: Weird.

The candelabras are raised, EDWARD watches them go up.

He looks out at the auditorium and takes the audience in.

He frowns, unsure of what is expected of him.

EDWARD: … I've had dreams like this. They never end well.

There is a loud crash behind him as GERTRUDE STEIN awkwardly navigates a door.

She is short and stout with closely cropped grey hair. She is in her sixties and is wearing a white shirt, with an embroidered waistcoat and broach, and a long woollen skirt. She has a commanding American voice.

Her entrance is hindered by the fact that she is astride a toilet. It's a modern toilet complete with pink fluffy toilet seat cover and matching footrest mat.

Eventually she settles. The door closes behind her.

GERTRUDE: *(Loud proclamation.)* I have arrived.

EDWARD: Okay.

GERTRUDE: Here I am.

EDWARD: Hi.

GERTRUDE: I am here.

EDWARD: Yes.

GERTRUDE: I am no longer there therefore I am here.

EDWARD: Well that's… good.

GERTRUDE: When I was there here was there but now I am here and there has become there for it is no longer here – it is there.

EDWARD: I see.

GERTRUDE: Do you?

EDWARD: No.

GERTRUDE: There is no here there there is only there there. Hence I am… *here.*

She looks around, a little uncertain of her surroundings.

EDWARD: You're very familiar.

GERTRUDE: I do not doubt it.

EDWARD: We've not met –?

GERTRUDE: I don't believe you've had the pleasure.

Beat.

EDWARD has a moment of recognition.

EDWARD: Wait. Are you –?

GERTRUDE: I am. I am I am I am I am I am.

EDWARD: Blimey.

GERTRUDE: I am… Am I?

EDWARD: Are you?

GERTRUDE: I am.

EDWARD: Right, gosh. What a treat.

Beat.

Can I ask –

GERTRUDE: I am a lion.

EDWARD: Okay.

GERTRUDE: I am a lion and I am poised. Poised I am as a lion as a lion as a lion as a lion I am poised, a lion I am. And I am for I am here. Here I am, a lion –

EDWARD: Poised.

She darts him a disgruntled look.

GERTRUDE: As a lion.

Small beat.

EDWARD: –

GERTRUDE: *(Renewed gusto.)* Resplendent in his field. A lion in his field resplendent. A lion lying in wait on his savannah.

EDWARD: *(Apologetically.)* Do you mind if I just –?

He circles behind her and tries to open the door she entered through – it is locked.

GERTRUDE is disgruntled by the interruption. She continues on whilst keeping a close eye on him –

GERTRUDE: A savannah his savannah the savannah Susanna on the savannah. A heat rises a child cries.

EDWARD stands downstage and looks out. Confused, he thinks.

A child cries for his mother Susanna his mother he cries.

GERTRUDE is losing patience with EDWARD's lack of engagement.

She gets louder, her delivery more intense in an attempt to secure his attention.

Susanna a mother a womb a womb a home a home no more expelled from his home a child cries for his mother.

EDWARD goes to an audience door. He tries to open it – it's locked.

Expelled from his home a child cries and the lion lies in wait.

EDWARD frowns to himself and goes to another audience door stage left – it is locked.

GERTRUDE: Here a lion and within her a womb – *(Furious.)* young man!

EDWARD stops in his tracks.

EDWARD: Me?

GERTRUDE: You.

EDWARD: Yes.

GERTRUDE: I am unaccustomed to such incessant fidgeting.

EDWARD: Sorry.

GERTRUDE: It is an impediment to civility /

EDWARD: Yes, sorry –

GERTRUDE: / and not the behaviour one has come to expect.

EDWARD: Sure, it's just –

GERTRUDE: Just what?

EDWARD: These doors –

GERTRUDE: Speak up!

EDWARD: The doors.

GERTRUDE: What of them?

EDWARD: They're shut.

GERTRUDE: *(Barely containing her rage.)* That is what doors do, young man, doors do shut.

EDWARD: *(Flustered.)* Yes but they do also do open.

GERTRUDE: I see we have a trickster in our midst. A jester... I am well aware that doors do open. They do open and they do close. That is their function.

EDWARD: These ones don't.

GERTRUDE: Don't what?

EDWARD: Open.

GERTRUDE: I have many interests, young man, but carpentry isn't one of them.

EDWARD: I think they're locked.

GERTRUDE: And what of it?

EDWARD: It's unusual.

GERTRUDE: Is it?

EDWARD: It's not standard.

GERTRUDE: Have you brought me here under the misguided notion that I am some sort of locksmith?

EDWARD: I haven't.

GERTRUDE: Good.

EDWARD: As in – I didn't.

GERTRUDE: Didn't what?

EDWARD: Bring you here.

GERTRUDE: Do you think I would come here of my own accord?

EDWARD: I haven't given it much thought.

GERTRUDE: *(Losing patience.)* What is here?

EDWARD: Good question.

GERTRUDE sighs, takes him in.

GERTRUDE: What am I here for?

EDWARD: What are you here for?

GERTRUDE: Whilst I usually encourage repetition, in daily discourse it very quickly becomes quite tiresome – for what purpose am I here?

EDWARD: You're asking me?

GERTRUDE: Whom else would I be asking?

EDWARD: I've no idea.

GERTRUDE narrows her eyes, suspicious of him.

Beat.

GERTRUDE: Where is Alice?

EDWARD: Alice?

GERTRUDE: Alice B. Toklas.

EDWARD: Of course.

GERTRUDE: Where is she?

EDWARD: I haven't seen her.

EDWARD moves downstage, looks out.

GERTRUDE: I never travel without her.

EDWARD: *(Distracted.)* That must be…confusing. Is it hot in here?

EDWARD takes off his jacket puts it on the stage.

GERTRUDE: I have the distinct impression you are not listening.

EDWARD: I'm so sorry. I absolutely am.

He looks out at the auditorium.

Beat.

GERTRUDE: What are you doing over there?

EDWARD: Having a little think.

GERTRUDE: What on?

EDWARD: We need to wait.

GERTRUDE: For what?

EDWARD: Direction.

GERTRUDE: From whom?

EDWARD: … Someone will come. Someone will come and they'll tell us what to do.

Beat.

I might be wrong but there are a few things that are a little…that just seem a bit…

He looks up at the ceiling, rubs his head.

GERTRUDE watches him, assessing him.

GERTRUDE: Who are you?

EDWARD is stumped.

EDWARD: I…erm. Well I'm –

GERTRUDE: What is your name?

EDWARD: It's, er –

He clicks his fingers trying to retrieve his name.

GERTRUDE: To whom am I speaking?

EDWARD: *(Baffled.)* I…

GERTRUDE: I can see you are determined to obfuscate.

EDWARD: I'm a little confused. I had a fall.

GERTRUDE: From grace?

EDWARD: It doesn't matter.

He looks out and waits.

Beat.

GERTRUDE: *(Growing concern.)* Where is she?

EDWARD: Who?

GERTRUDE: You don't listen.

EDWARD: I'm trying. There's a lot going on.

GERTRUDE: Alice B. Toklas.

EDWARD: Yes.

GERTRUDE: My wife.

EDWARD: Yes.

GERTRUDE: My beloved. I'm looking for her.

EDWARD: That's right.

GERTRUDE: I should like to know her whereabouts.

EDWARD: I'm sure she'll turn up.

GERTRUDE: I never travel without her.

EDWARD: You said.

GERTRUDE: She'll have my itinerary.

EDWARD: That'd be handy.

GERTRUDE: You haven't seen her?

EDWARD: I haven't.

He goes back to waiting.

GERTRUDE sighs.

Beat.

She leans back in her 'chair' regally.

GERTRUDE: You've made no provisions for my arrival.

EDWARD: No.

GERTRUDE: I am not even blessed with a decent chair.

EDWARD: I'm sorry I wasn't expecting you.

GERTRUDE: It's a sad day indeed when one finds oneself longing for a firm stool –

She attempts to lean her elbow on the cistern, she misses and hits the toilet handle, it flushes loudly.

GERTRUDE looks down at her seat with abject horror.

She looks slowly back up at EDWARD.

GERTRUDE: *(Stern disbelief.)* What was that?

EDWARD: It sounded like a flush.

GERTRUDE: A flush? And why, may I ask, is my chair –

GERTRUDE looks down at her chair, back up to EDWARD.

Young man, am I to understand that you have me straddling – a john?

EDWARD: It's not my doing –

GERTRUDE: A lavatory?

EDWARD: It's possible.

Beat.

GERTRUDE laughs uproariously. It's a great, open, free laugh.

GERTRUDE: You've got balls I'll give you that.

EDWARD: Right. This isn't my doing.

GERTRUDE: *(Still laughing.)* You've got me on a – what is it, a commode?

EDWARD: *(Flustered.)* I had nothing to do with –

GERTRUDE: A latrine!

EDWARD: You came in on it.

GERTRUDE: How progressive of me.

EDWARD: You brought it with you.

GERTRUDE: *(Enjoying herself.)* Alice will die when she hears of it, she will simply die! Where is she?

EDWARD: I don't know. I've only just arrived myself.

GERTRUDE: And what did you come in on – a refrigerator?

EDWARD: No –

GERTRUDE: A bed?

EDWARD: No –

GERTRUDE: I know, I know – a…don't tell me – in a bathtub?

EDWARD: No, I didn't come in or on anything.

GERTRUDE: You didn't?

EDWARD: I landed.

GERTRUDE: Landed? From where?

EDWARD points to the ceiling.

EDWARD: Up there.

GERTRUDE: How marvellous!

EDWARD: It wasn't intentional.

GERTRUDE: *(Not listening.)* So festive.

EDWARD: It just happened. I fell.

GERTRUDE is unable to see a hole in the ceiling.

GERTRUDE: I don't see how.

EDWARD: You don't see how, I don't see why.

GERTRUDE: I rarely find chasing *why* produces satisfactory
results, much better to simply say *because* and get on with it.

EDWARD tries to open the central main door again – it is locked.

EDWARD: Someone will be along soon. They'll give us
direction and everything will start to make sense –

*Two doors open; out of one enters a man dressed in leathers with
a handlebar moustache, out of the other enters a man dressed as
a cowboy (à la Village People) they enter the space and cross the
stage with purpose.*

EDWARD watches dumbfounded.

GERTRUDE is delighted.

GERTRUDE: Hello boys!

As the men pass they give GERTRUDE a cursory nod.

LEATHER MAN: Alright?   COWBOY: Hiya.

EDWARD, speechless, manages a small wave.

As the men pass EDWARD they mumble –

LEATHER MAN: Loser.   COWBOY: Fatso.

EDWARD looks after them quizzically, unsure if he heard right.

The men exit via opposite doors to the ones they entered. The doors shut behind them.

GERTRUDE: This place is a hoot!

Beat.

EDWARD: Something's definitely not right. Things aren't –

He rouses himself and runs to check the door one of the men went through – it's locked.

GERTRUDE: Isn't it fun?

EDWARD: I don't like it.

GERTRUDE: Oh, relax.

EDWARD: I'm unsettled. I find it unsettling.

EDWARD goes over and checks the other door – it is locked.

GERTRUDE picks up his jacket, looks inside it.

GERTRUDE: Edward the Second.

EDWARD: What's that?

GERTRUDE: Edward the Second.

EDWARD: That rings a bell.

GERTRUDE: Well it would.

EDWARD: Would it?

GERTRUDE: It should.

EDWARD: Should it?

GERTRUDE: It's your name.

EDWARD: How d'you know?

GERTRUDE: It's written on the inside of your jacket.

EDWARD: I see.

She turns the jacket around for him to see the label.

EDWARD: I guess that makes sense then.

GERTRUDE: Sense is overrated.

He picks up the jacket and looks at the name.

EDWARD: But this door situation –

GERTRUDE: Not this again.

He hugs his jacket for comfort.

EDWARD: Something's not right.

EDWARD runs down and checks the central audience door – it's locked.

GERTRUDE: I refuse to indulge this needless fretting.

EDWARD: It doesn't worry you?

GERTRUDE: Doors that can be locked, can always be unlocked.

Beat.

EDWARD: I think it's queer.

QUENTIN: *(Off.)* And it's about to get queerer.

The ceiling hatch opens and QUENTIN CRISP is lowered slowly down on a giant swing.

He's in his sixties and is wearing a suit with an extravagant floral necktie, a hat sits stylishly askew on his head and his fingers are adorned with large rings.

The swing stops in front of the musicians' gallery.

Beat.

QUENTIN is unsteady, nervous of the height.

EDWARD looks up.

EDWARD: … You alright?

QUENTIN: *(Not alright.)* Marvellous.

GERTRUDE claps her hands together enthusiastically.

GERTRUDE: Who have we now?

QUENTIN: Mr Crisp.

GERTRUDE: Quentin?

QUENTIN: The very same.

EDWARD: … Right.

EDWARD is confused, lost in thought.

GERTRUDE: How wonderful. What fun. Welcome!

QUENTIN: Thank you. Where am I?

GERTRUDE: As to that, I'm afraid we're unclear.

QUENTIN: To whom am I speaking? I daren't look down.

GERTRUDE: It's Gertrude.

QUENTIN: Forgive me, I seem to be at odds with the ground.

GERTRUDE: He's got you on a swing.

QUENTIN: So I gather. How unfortunate.

GERTRUDE: Of course he'll swear blind it isn't his doing.

EDWARD: It isn't my doing.

GERTRUDE: You see?

QUENTIN: Are you on firmer footing down there?

GERTRUDE: I'm on the lavatory.

QUENTIN: Well, when you've got to go you've got to go.

GERTRUDE: Quite so. However in this instance I'm not compelled here by my own internal stirrings, but rather by the will of our young friend here. To what end – he won't say.

EDWARD: I've nothing to do with any of this.

GERTRUDE: You'll find him quite repetitive, and not in a good way.

QUENTIN: Is he handsome? I can't see.

GERTRUDE: Not particularly. His name is Edward the Second.

QUENTIN: How very grand. What happened to the first?

GERTRUDE: I've no idea. But this one's afraid of doors.

EDWARD: I'm not afraid of them, I'd just like to be able to use them.

QUENTIN: Doors are a distant concern at present. I'd be more partial to pursuing some sort of purchase.

GERTRUDE: Do you feel stable?

QUENTIN: Not in the least.

GERTRUDE: Your natural poise will keep you aloft.

QUENTIN: We can only hope. I've never seen the value in elevation.

EDWARD: What can you see up there?

QUENTIN: Nothing of worth. What were you hoping for?

EDWARD: I don't know – some answers?

QUENTIN: One is always taught to believe that a bird's eye view will provide some attractive perspective or clarity. I'm sad to report that, in this case, neither is true. On account of the fact that I'm too shit scared to look.

Beat.

Curious.

EDWARD: Which bit?

QUENTIN: I never curse.

GERTRUDE: I've been misquoting myself since I arrived.

QUENTIN: And curiouser.

EDWARD points to the ceiling.

EDWARD: What's up there?

QUENTIN: I haven't the faintest.

EDWARD: You just came from there.

GERTRUDE: As did you.

QUENTIN: I seem to have materialised here.

EDWARD: I fell.

GERTRUDE: I came in on a toilet.

QUENTIN: Perhaps you're a fallen angel?

GERTRUDE: Highly doubtful – he lacks any sort of grace.

QUENTIN: Why am I on this – swing?

EDWARD: I've no idea.

QUENTIN: I've never swung in my life.

GERTRUDE: Have you not?

QUENTIN: It's unseemly.

GERTRUDE: Believe you me, it could be worse.

QUENTIN: Yes, what a predicament he's got us both in.

GERTRUDE: At least we're sat.

QUENTIN: True.

GERTRUDE: My toilet is adorned with pink carpet. Have you ever seen such a thing?

QUENTIN: Piggy pink or pale?

GERTRUDE: Fuchsia.

QUENTIN: How delightfully garish.

GERTRUDE: I cannot fathom the purpose of such frilly embellishments.

EDWARD: Splashback.

GERTRUDE: *(Stern.)* I beg your pardon?

EDWARD: If you – if one…misses. It's absorbed by the carpet.

Beat.

GERTRUDE: How alarming that thus far this is the only thing you are willing to answer with any sense of clarity… And for the record I am not in the habit of 'missing.'

EDWARD: *(To QUENTIN.)* Listen, someone will be along soon and they'll get you down. I'm sure it won't be long.

QUENTIN: One feels like one has spent one's whole life hanging by a thread over a precipice with an audience gawping at me.

EDWARD: Hmmm.

QUENTIN: Do I detect discomfort?

EDWARD: No, it's just – I'm trying to ignore that they're here. Things are complicated enough as it is.

QUENTIN: One must never not embrace an audience.

He beams and opens his arms to the audience. He becomes unsteady.

Oh –

EDWARD: What?

QUENTIN: I nearly swung.

GERTRUDE: Careful.

QUENTIN: It won't happen again. *(To GERTRUDE.)* What has he told you?

GERTRUDE: He says he doesn't know anything –

EDWARD: I don't.

GERTRUDE: You see? It's become remarkably easy to predict what he'll say next.

EDWARD: I feel a bit light headed.

QUENTIN: Put your head between your knees. *(To GERTRUDE.)* Has he told you why we were summoned?

GERTRUDE: You weren't.   EDWARD: You weren't.

EDWARD looks at GERTRUDE, disconcerted.

GERTRUDE: You weren't   EDWARD: You weren't
summoned. At least   summoned. At least
not by me.   not by me.

EDWARD looks at GERTRUDE who smiles cheekily.

GERTRUDE: *(To QUENTIN.)* You see?

QUENTIN: I do. Fun.

QUENTIN joins GERTRUDE in her game.

ALL: It isn't fun.

Beat.

ALL: I don't like it.

Beat.

EDWARD is becoming flustered.

ALL: How are you doing this?

GERTRUDE and QUENTIN laugh uproariously, they clap their hands together.

EDWARD glares at them.

ALL: You can stop it now.

ALL: You've proved your point.

ALL: …You're making me sweat!

QUENTIN and GERTRUDE are becoming feverish with enjoyment.

EDWARD is beginning to panic.

They talk faster.

ALL: This isn't right.

ALL: None of this is making sense.

EDWARD tries to frantically open the central audience door again.

ALL: Why won't these doors open?

ALL: I want to get out!

QUENTIN and GERTRUDE laugh hysterically.

Suddenly there is a fierce banging from the other side of the central audience door.

The three of them stop.

They watch the door nervously.

The banging returns and the door rattles violently.

EDWARD backs slowly away from the door.

Beat.

QUENTIN: You want to get out but something wants to get in.

EDWARD: What is it?

GERTRUDE: It's here for you.

QUENTIN: It's you it wants.

They both stare at him gravely.

QUENTIN: There's something amiss here.

EDWARD: You're telling me.

QUENTIN: I can smell it.

GERTRUDE: Yes.

QUENTIN: Taste it.

GERTRUDE: Quite so.

EDWARD: What? What can you taste?

QUENTIN: Things are not what they seem.

EDWARD: No shit!

GERTRUDE: We're there aren't we?

EDWARD: Where?

GERTRUDE: The neither here nor there.

QUENTIN: In the between and the betwixt.

EDWARD: What does that mean?

GERTRUDE: We're stuck.

QUENTIN: And it's his doing.

They look at EDWARD.

EDWARD looks up at them nervously.

EDWARD: I want to be here even less than you do.

HARVEY MILK appears. He is in his forties. He's wearing a respectable 1970's suit and tie. He has an upbeat zany quality, a can-do disposition.

He shouts down a tin megaphone –

HARVEY: My name is Harvey Milk and I want to recruit you!

He approaches EDWARD.

HARVEY: You.

EDWARD: Me?

HARVEY: Are you a homosexual?

EDWARD: Yes.

HARVEY: Thatta boy!

EDWARD: Don't tell me this is normal.

HARVEY: What?

EDWARD: You being here.

HARVEY: I wouldn't dream of it.

QUENTIN: I don't think normal is on any of our agendas.

GERTRUDE: It's not a word that sits in my lexicon.

HARVEY: I sense fellow degenerates, and I like it.

QUENTIN: It would appear we're all of a wonky persuasion.

HARVEY: Then we're in fine company!

GERTRUDE: *(Gleefully.)* It's like the old days of the salon.

QUENTIN: It's possible I've been to worse parties.

GERTRUDE: Alice would love this.

EDWARD: I'm a homosexual. Why do I know that but not my own name?

HARVEY: What is your name?

EDWARD: My jacket says Edward the Second.

HARVEY: You're adorable.

He produces a carton of popcorn.

Break it down for me Eddie, can I call you Eddie? Who're your friends?

EDWARD: Gertrude Stein is on the toilet, Quentin Crisp is on the swing.

HARVEY: Naturally.

He tosses a piece of popcorn in the air and catches it in his mouth.

GERTRUDE: Good evening.

QUENTIN: How do you do?

HARVEY: *(Down the haler.)* My name is Harvey Milk and I want to recruit you!

QUENTIN: Yes, we heard you the first time.

HARVEY: *(To GERTRUDE.)* It's always nice to meet a fellow American abroad.

GERTRUDE: We certainly are that here.

HARVEY: American?

GERTRUDE: Abroad.

QUENTIN: Adrift.

GERTRUDE: Exiled.

EDWARD: *(To HARVEY.)* They'll have you believe that I brought you here.

HARVEY: Well kid, you did.

EDWARD: I didn't! Why would I?

HARVEY: Don't sweat it Eddie, you'll figure it.

He throws another piece of popcorn and catches it in his mouth.

QUENTIN: What exactly are you hoping to recruit us for?

HARVEY: The cause.

QUENTIN: We're a little past causes.

They begin to increasingly vie for EDWARD's attention.

GERTRUDE: I only wish my Alice were here.

HARVEY: *(Down the haler.)* To win our right to self-respect and equality, we must first assert our full existence and strength.

QUENTIN: Assert by all means, but don't shout.

EDWARD: *(To GERTRUDE.)* I'm sure she'll be here soon.

GERTRUDE: I never travel without her.

HARVEY: *(To EDWARD.)* Are you out?

EDWARD: I think so.

HARVEY: We must all come out –

QUENTIN: That ship has long since sailed. The jig is up.

HARVEY: To our neighbours, our fellow workers, the people who work where we eat and shop –

QUENTIN: *(To EDWARD.)* I'm not sure I've ever even seen a closet.

GERTRUDE: She'll have my itinerary. She is quite meticulous. She is full-thoughtful.

HARVEY: *(Still down the haler.)* We must band together and fight straight oppression.

QUENTIN: There is never a need to shout.

HARVEY drops his haler.

HARVEY: You've been loud in your time Mr Crisp.

QUENTIN: Present, persistent, in full view, but never loud.

GERTRUDE: She is full-thoughtful and full of thought.

HARVEY: We have a lot to shout about, right Eddie?

GERTRUDE: I am I because she knows me.[1]

QUENTIN: Much better to bore people into submission. Quietly show up and let them plainly see you exist.

GERTRUDE: I am I yes Madame am I I.

QUENTIN: Constantly present yourself to them in their everyday lives. Consistency moves mountains.

GERTRUDE: I am I because she knows me.

QUENTIN: Then they will see and they will say to themselves – here is one out shopping, as I am out shopping. He eats and drinks as I do eat and drink. Here he is doing no harm.

---

1   Loosely inspired by Gertrude Stein's passage 'I am I because my little dog knows me' from *The Geographical History of America* (1936).

GERTRUDE: When I am I am I I

HARVEY: Some of us need the mountain to move a little faster.

GERTRUDE: And I am I because she knows me I am I I

EDWARD goes to inspect the central audience door.

EDWARD: Maybe it was Alice that was knocking?

GERTRUDE: Whatever that was, that was not Alice.

HARVEY: Knocking?

QUENTIN: There was rather a loud banging on that door.

He points it out to HARVEY.

GERTRUDE: Alice B. Toklas has a temper but she is always a
lady. That was no lady.

QUENTIN: Something wanted in. It was quite ferocious.

HARVEY: Was it the cops?

EDWARD: *(Alarmed.)* The cops?

QUENTIN: In my experience the police rarely afford one the
courtesy of knocking.

EDWARD: We're not doing anything wrong –

HARVEY: Three queers and a lesbian amounts to a
congregation.

QUENTIN: It sounded more like 'roughs'. But they hunt in
packs of course.

HARVEY: Eddie there's enough here to raid a club, arrest the
patrons.

EDWARD: We're just waiting to be told what to do.

HARVEY: Charge us as 'inmates of a disorderly house'.

They compete and vie for EDWARD's attention with growing intensity.

QUENTIN: Bounding through Soho, police on our left, roughs on our right and us springing down Old Compton Street like startled gazelles.

HARVEY: We had a system, if a cop walked into a bar we'd flick the lights on and off –

QUENTIN: We moved as a herd. Bound together by a constant danger, splitting apart when the chase was on –

HARVEY: We'd flick the lights on and off and all the dancers would quickly swap partners –

QUENTIN: Scattering ourselves wide down darkened alleyways.

HARVEY: The lesbians pairing up and dancing with the gay men.

QUENTIN: We were a collection of lost souls randomly tossed together in the gutter, struggling for survival.

GERTRUDE: Surround oneself with the right people and one need never struggle again.

HARVEY: Dancing together under flickering lights – a spectacle of normality.

GERTRUDE: Matisse, Picasso, Hemmingway, Cezanne, Fitzgerald – all in our little dining room. *(To EDWARD.)* Can you imagine such a thing?

QUENTIN: They despised me of course, the other Queens.

GERTRUDE: We were only ever ourselves, Alice and I, ourselves were we only.

QUENTIN: I was too much of a giveaway for the closets, you see. Too effeminate.

33

GERTRUDE: She'd sit in the kitchen with the wives of other geniuses, waiting patiently for me, while I discoursed with the men.

QUENTIN: I was like an unwanted siren, a lighthouse flashing enemy ships – here be queers! Here be queers!

GERTRUDE: My baby, my queen, my lobster, my wifey.

Overwhelmed, EDWARD turns away from them.

EDWARD: *(To himself.)* Inmates of a disorderly house.

GERTRUDE stands abruptly on her toilet seat, she addresses EDWARD and the audience –

GERTRUDE: An earthquake brought her to me.

HARVEY: San Francisco, 1906.

HARVEY drums his hands on his knees.

EDWARD turns back to face them.

GERTRUDE: She stood barefoot at dawn and watched as the soil beneath her feet convulsed. The ground urgently heralding change, trembling with the promise of a new life.

HARVEY's drumming reaches a crescendo.

HARVEY: She looked out at her humbled city.

GERTRUDE: She took stock of her broken structures.

HARVEY: She knew her world to be cracked open.

There is a faint sound of voices singing off stage, it's delicate and beautiful.

GERTRUDE: She knew she had to leave.

HARVEY: She boarded a ship.

GERTRUDE: And began her voyage her voyage her voyage to me.

HARVEY: You sat patiently waiting –

GERTRUDE: In the living room of my brother's house. Waiting waiting I was.

HARVEY: The Parisian sun glared through the large windows.

GERTRUDE: I waiting sat waiting unaware that what I was waiting for was her.

HARVEY: The great grand door opened and in she walked –

GERTRUDE: Alice. My Alice –

GERTRUDE turns toward QUENTIN and gestures to him.

He motions to himself – 'me?'

GERTRUDE nods.

QUENTIN repositions himself on his swing. They look at each other.

QUENTIN: You were sat in a large armchair. Dressed in a warm brown corduroy suit. You were a golden presence burned by the sun.

GERTRUDE smiles warmly at him.

You had a large coral broach pinned to your lapel. And when you spoke I felt sure that your voice came from this broach. When I looked at you I heard bells ringing and I knew that I was in the presence of a genius.[2]

We hear the faint sound of distant bells ringing.

GERTRUDE: You learnt to type up my manuscripts on an old Blickensderfer.

---

2   Loosely based on Alice B. Toklas' account in *What is Remembered* (1963).

QUENTIN: I played your words on it. My fingers adapted to your work. It was like playing Bach.

GERTRUDE: You cooked me American food with all the Californian flavours I'd been missing.

QUENTIN: Chicken fricassee, roast turkey stuffed with mushrooms, cornbread, apple and lemon pies.

GERTRUDE: We kicked off our sandals.

QUENTIN: And climbed a mountain.

GERTRUDE: Breathless and giddy we reached the top.

QUENTIN: I unpacked the sandwiches I'd made us and you turned to me and said –

GERTRUDE: I have been very happy today.

GERTRUDE has tears in her eyes.

Beat.

QUENTIN: You asked me to be your bride.

GERTRUDE reaches out her hand to QUENTIN.

You were to be my husband.

QUENTIN reaches out his hand to GERTRUDE – they're too far apart to touch.

GERTRUDE: And you my wife.

They reach out across the space for each other.

The trap in the floor flies open, breaking the magic. The singing stops.

Slowly a figure ascends and stands upright in the trap. From this position she looks out at the audience and surveys them with a steely stare.

It's MARGARET THATCHER. Her bouffant hair perfectly set, she's wearing a blue jacket and skirt, large pearl earrings and necklace, a blue silk scarf is tied around her neck in a perfect bow.

The others stare at her with nervous expectancy.

Beat.

She speaks very slowly, softly and willfully. She has an other-worldly, unnerving energy.

THATCHER: I have something to say.

EDWARD: … No.

She whips around viciously and stares at EDWARD.

THATCHER: I have some things that I should like to say.

EDWARD: No. I'm sorry. This is too much.

He walks toward the trap.

I'm going to have to ask you to leave.

THATCHER: But I have some things that I'd like to say.

EDWARD: No thank you.

He lifts up the trap door.

Off you go, please?

She stares at him as she slowly makes her way back down.

That's it. Thank you.

THATCHER: Are you sure about this, young man?

EDWARD: Quite sure. Thanks all the same. Mind your head.

She disappears below.

Are you all clear?

THATCHER's hand appears through the trap and gives a thumbs up.

EDWARD: Out the way then.

He slams the door shut.

Uncomfortable beat.

EDWARD stares at the trap.

GERTRUDE gets down from her toilet.

QUENTIN shifts uncomfortably on the swing.

HARVEY sorrowfully eats his popcorn.

QUENTIN: Even a rudimentary understanding of manners will permit a guest to speak.

EDWARD: I don't want to hear the things she has to say.

HARVEY: I didn't like her jive.

QUENTIN: Has it occurred to you that she may have been offering a way out?

GERTRUDE: She might have known where Alice was.

EDWARD: She didn't. She wasn't.

QUENTIN: She might've been able to get me down.

EDWARD: She wasn't about to hand you a step-ladder – believe me.

QUENTIN: Even if her discourse lacked information, it would've at least been interesting.

EDWARD: She has nothing interesting to say.

QUENTIN: I disagree.

EDWARD looks at him.

QUENTIN: I have no fear in telling you that I find her rather marvellous.

EDWARD: *What?*

QUENTIN: Anyone so unconcerned with being loved has my full admiration.

EDWARD: She's against everything you stood for.

QUENTIN: I never stood, I walked. Head high, shoulders back, eyes front and at a speed of five miles per hour. Stand still and you invite trouble. Stand still and the world will wallop you in the face.

GERTRUDE: You're speaking figuratively?

QUENTIN: I assure you I'm being quite literal – I've been slapped at many a bus stop.

EDWARD: *(To QUENTIN.)* She'd get rid of every single one of us if she could.

QUENTIN: Don't be hysterical.

Beat. They all contemplate Edward's thought.

QUENTIN points to the hatch.

QUENTIN: That may have been our only way out.

EDWARD: Shit!

EDWARD rushes to the hatch and tries to open it. It is locked.

They all look at the closed hatch despondently.

QUENTIN: *(Softly, contemplatively.)* There is no getting rid of us, we've been here since time immemorial. We were at it in the caves.

GERTRUDE claps her hands together enthusiastically.

GERTRUDE: Those charming drawings they discovered in China.

HARVEY and GERTRUDE begin to rally throughout the following, they try to engage EDWARD who is staring glumly at the trap.

HARVEY: The prehistoric porn?

GERTRUDE: Yes, those wonderful petroglyphs – all those men and women delighting in each other's bodies.

HARVEY: The earliest known pornography – not what the archaeologists had in mind I bet.

GERTRUDE: Little moments of joy etched in stone.

HARVEY: There they are ploughing away at dry, salty desert sands for months – years! And what do they find? Porn!

GERTRUDE: The small shaking hand of the artist, his eyes narrowing, his lips contorting with concentration.

HARVEY: Men with giant phalluses, women with shapely hips and long legs.

QUENTIN: Their right palm pointing up to the sky, their left hand down indicating the earth.

QUENTIN demonstrates this.

HARVEY: All frantically dancing in a circle.

GERTRUDE grabs EDWARD and spins him joyfully.

GERTRUDE: And among them a third group –

QUENTIN: Adorned with the sign of women but themselves sporting pulsating –

GERTRUDE: Bisexuals!

HARVEY: Lesbians, Gays, Bisexuals, Transsexuals and Queers – yes, we've been here for years!

QUENTIN: I wonder if the diggers blushed.

HARVEY: Imagine their horror – not only did they dig up
porn but it was also *(To EDWARD.)* to use the lingo of your
time – bi-curious!

QUENTIN: *(Disdainfully.)* This distasteful desire for labels.

HARVEY: Freely loving and dancing under fountains of semen.

*GERTRUDE stops spinning EDWARD and sits back on her toilet,
disgruntled and out of breath.*

GERTRUDE: Prosaic pieces, of course, but not without their
charm.

HARVEY: All those years hidden under rock and sand, silently
spinning in their circles in the dark.

QUENTIN: *(Wistfully.)* Fumbling and falling in the gloom.
Clandestine adventures round darkened corners. Looking
for tenderness down urine-stained alleyways.

HARVEY: *(Reminiscing.)* Crammed into butcher's trucks.
Hauling meat around the city by day, left open at night
for us to congregate, touch, enjoy each other. We'd step
up into the dark, enter the open backs of these stinking
vehicles and reach out...

QUENTIN: How positively carnal.

HARVEY: The smell of meat, the warmth of flesh.

EDWARD: I'm still in those trucks.

QUENTIN: You can't be.

GERTRUDE: You're not.

HARVEY: You never were.

EDWARD: I feel like I am.

GERTRUDE: He's either being metaphorical or obtuse.

HARVEY: We were there because we were tired of getting busted in bars.

QUENTIN: *(To EDWARD.)* You have no such concerns.

EDWARD: I can't describe it.

HARVEY: You feel like you're hiding?

EDWARD: Not hiding, no.

HARVEY: Being held back.

EDWARD: Yes, maybe.

QUENTIN: By what?

GERTRUDE: Everything is available to you.

HARVEY: All those laws.

QUENTIN: All that transparency.

HARVEY: *(Wistfully.)* All that sex.

He chews his popcorn dreamily.

EDWARD: I don't feel free.

GERTRUDE: *(To EDWARD.)* I find you ungrateful.

QUENTIN: It would appear progression doesn't buy happiness.

Behind their backs, a door opens. MARGARET THATCHER enters, the door quickly shuts behind her. She looks a bit dishevelled, her hair is a little messy. She surreptitiously edges her way round the back of the stage.

HARVEY: *(To EDWARD.)* Aren't you happy?

GERTRUDE: *(Sternly to EDWARD.)* You should be happier.

HARVEY: *(To EDWARD.)* Are you getting any?

QUENTIN: It's so readily available now.

EDWARD: But it lacks intimacy.

HARVEY: There was no intimacy in the trucks, if there was it was fleeting, a by-product. And if you got it, you held onto it for weeks.

GERTRUDE: Intimacy is what you want?

EDWARD: I think so, yes.

QUENTIN: *(To himself.)* Tenderness.

HARVEY: Intimacy is hard to find when you don't think you're worthy of it.

EDWARD: … Do you think that's what my –?

He turns to look at them all, spots THATCHER. He jumps.

EDWARD: Jesus! No. *Out.*

He points for her to leave.

THATCHER skittishly bolts for a door, the door closes quickly behind her.

QUENTIN: She'll be back.

EDWARD: If she is, I'll send her out again.

EDWARD and QUENTIN share a look – a small stand-off between them.

EDWARD turns away.

QUENTIN: Sex has always been a murky business. No matter what you're up to or with whom, we're all taught to regret it.

GERTRUDE: The Fall of Man, the death of Eden.

QUENTIN: Quite so. We're meant to spend our lives atoning for the mistakes they made in that great grand garden of theirs, not following our base desires in the back of meat trucks.

HARVEY: Golly, it was fun though.

He eats his popcorn, lost in memories.

QUENTIN: Anything beyond procreation and they won't allow it. As long as no one's enjoying themselves they'll turn a blind eye. Even the straights don't have it easy, they're not permitted to live it up either.

GERTRUDE: *(Musing.)* When all is said one is wedded to bed.[3]

QUENTIN: Of course I sidestepped any guilt by charging for it. If I was being paid then I was working, therefore the exchange was for profit and not for joy. I thought even he *(Indicates God above.)* would allow me that logic.

GERTRUDE: *(Increasingly feverish.)* Have it as having having it as happening, happening to have it as happening, having to have it as happening. Happening and have it as happening and having to have it happen as happening *(She closes her eyes, grips her toilet for support.)* and my wife has a cow as now, my wife having a cow as now, my wife having a cow as now, my wife having a cow as now and having a cow as now and having a cow and having a cow and having a cow now, my wife has a cow and now. My wife has a cow.[4]

GERTRUDE slumps back in a post-orgasmic heap on her toilet.

Beat.

The others stare at her silently.

---

3   From *The Autobiography of Alice B. Toklas*, by Gertrude Stein (1933).
4   From *A Book Concluding With As a Wife Has a Cow: A Love Story*, by Gertrude Stein (1926).

HARVEY: Golly.

QUENTIN: Gosh.

EDWARD: No one's ever made me *moo*.

QUENTIN: Me neither.

HARVEY: Oh there was Terry, Scottie, Stew, Gareth, Mark, Sebastian –

He leans back and rests his head in his hands, pleasantly lost in his memories.

John, James, Matthew, and then Kevin of course, Kenny, Mikey, Stevie –

EDWARD looks glumly out at the auditorium as HARVEY's list continues.

EDWARD: No one's coming are they? No one good I mean. No one to get us out.

A door opens, DOROTHY GALE enters in a plaid dress and ruby slippers, hair in plaits. She skips merrily through the space. When she reaches EDWARD she stops, hoicks up phlegm, spits in his face, then skips merrily out of a door. The door shuts behind her.

EDWARD looks out dumbfounded.

EDWARD: If I didn't know better, I could start to get really paranoid.

THATCHER appears in the upper gallery amongst the audience. She's a little more dishevelled again – her silk scarf has come undone, her shirt untucked, her hair is messier still.

QUENTIN: She's up here look. Lady T!

He points and waves, the others look.

EDWARD: What now?

HARVEY: Don't worry, she's not well lit. No one can see her up there.

THATCHER produces a lit hand-held candle.

QUENTIN: *(In admiration.)* She's brought her own candle. She thinks of everything!

THATCHER: I have something to say.

EDWARD: Oh here we go.

THATCHER addresses the whole auditorium.

THATCHER: It is the predicament of our boys and girls that concerns me most. Too often they don't receive the education they require.

EDWARD: I've heard this speech before.

THATCHER: *(To EDWARD.)* It is the 1987 Conservative Party conference. Do not interrupt me, I am on a roll. Too often they don't receive the education they require, the education they deserve.

EDWARD: I was five.

THATCHER: Our boys and girls who need to learn to respect traditional moral values are being instructed to believe they have an unassailable right to be gay. Our boys and girls are being cheated of a proper start in life… Yes, cheated.

She looks around, waiting for applause.

EDWARD looks to QUENTIN.

QUENTIN: Not one of her best, I'll give you that.

EDWARD: This was the start of –

THATCHER: Section 28. I'll accept this interruption because it's an important point. Section 28 – an amendment passed through the House of Commons with an enthusiastic majority on 24th May 1987.

EDWARD: I was in infant school.

HARVEY: You liked drawing sunsets.

THATCHER: A flagship moment for our country, for our party, and most importantly for me personally.

HARVEY: *(To EDWARD.)* Your best friend was Darren.

THATCHER: *(Proud.)* The message reverberated joyously throughout the land.

HARVEY: *(To EDWARD.)* You wanted his approval more than anything.

THATCHER: Local authorities shall not intentionally promote homosexuality or publish material with the intention of promoting homosexuality.

HARVEY: *(To EDWARD.)* Your belly went funny when he was nice to you.

THATCHER: Or promote the teaching in any maintained school of the acceptability of homosexuality as a pretended family relationship.

EDWARD looks accusingly to QUENTIN.

QUENTIN: *(To EDWARD.)* Heterosexuals rule the world, what did you expect her to say?

EDWARD and THATCHER stare at each other.

THATCHER: I regret nothing.

Beat.

EDWARD: Is that everything?

THATCHER shakes her head –

THATCHER: No.

EDWARD: *(Ignoring her.)* Great. You know your way out.

THATCHER: But –

EDWARD: *(To an audience member.)* Could you blow her candle out please?

The audience member does.

EDWARD: Thank you.

Crestfallen, THATCHER leaves.

GERTRUDE: The last time I was in a room as strange as this Alice had over-egged the hash brownies and Pablo was sick in his shoe.

EDWARD looks accusingly at QUENTIN.

QUENTIN: I'm not here to please anyone.

EDWARD: She's a vile, sub-human creature –

QUENTIN: How reductive! How reactionary!

EDWARD: And I lose respect for anyone that thinks otherwise.

QUENTIN: She stood for individualism. For striving for what you believe in.

EDWARD: Her policies were devastating.

QUENTIN: Legislation means nothing.

HARVEY: What the hell?

QUENTIN: It is the will of the people that matters.

HARVEY: Change comes from the top down.

QUENTIN: If there is a policy they do not like, the great British public will ignore it, subvert it. So it is the minds of the people that need to change, show the people who you are and the rest will follow suit.

HARVEY: I'm all for individualism if it means allowing people to be themselves but it is society's duty to provide and shelter, to offer a safe and equal space to all individuals, regardless of race, gender or sexuality.

GERTRUDE: Some of us are happy to fend for ourselves, to be left alone.

HARVEY: *(To GERTRUDE.)* And yet you crave attention as much as any of us.

GERTRUDE: I am happy to live within that contradiction.

QUENTIN: Homosexuals are by their very nature inward looking. Self-protectionist.

EDWARD: What?

HARVEY: We are not.

QUENTIN: We've had to be.

GERTRUDE: Survival by any means necessary.

QUENTIN: We seek first to look after ourselves, only then do we think of our friends and then our families.

EDWARD: That's not true.

GERTRUDE: It got Alice and I through two world wars as well as countless dinner parties.

QUENTIN: It is rare that our outlook exceeds beyond the confines of own existence.

HARVEY: Then sir, consider me an anomaly.

EDWARD: Me too.

QUENTIN: *(To EDWARD.)* And yet what is there here in this very room that breaches your own limited perspective?

EDWARD flounders.

EDWARD: *(To QUENTIN.)* The things you're saying are old fashioned, they're out of date.

QUENTIN: Be careful.

EDWARD: They don't represent me.

QUENTIN: You're judging us through the prism of your own time. It is an advantage not afforded to us all.

Beat.

HARVEY claps his hands together excitedly.

HARVEY: *(Gusto.)* San Francisco. 1951. The Black Cat Café. The best gay bar in America!

He removes his jacket and rolls up his sleeves.

The last orders at the bar have been called. The small but mighty José Sarria – cabaret star, political activist, drag Empress – in a glittering sequined dress...

He grabs a scarf or shawl from an audience member, drapes it around himself.

Stands on top of a table and addresses the crowd –

He stands on higher footing.

(As José.) I want you all to remember that there is nothing wrong in being gay, the crime is getting caught. United we stand, divided they catch us one by one. I want you all to stand up.

GERTRUDE and EDWARD stand, QUENTIN puts his hand over his heart. They face out.

HARVEY: For one moment I want you to stand here and be proud of who you are.

Beat.

HARVEY begins singing, voices backstage join in –

God save us Nelly Queens,

Long Live us Nelly Queens,

God save us Queens.

(And lesbians too.)

The backstage chorus continue humming.

HARVEY: José led the singing bar out onto the street. They stood shoulder to shoulder and sang up to The Old Hall of Justice across the road. Up to the gay tier.

They all look up to the Upper Gallery.

HARVEY: Where the men who'd been arrested that day looked down from their cell windows at the crowd singing proudly up to them. The men who were there that night in those cells said they'd never forgotten it, that they knew, for a fleeting moment, that they were not alone.

All on stage and backstage sing triumphantly –

ALL: From every mountainside,

Long may you love or fly,

God save us Nelly Queens,

God save us Queens!

Beat.

QUENTIN: That's not been my experience.

The magic of the moment is broken.

HARVEY looks at QUENTIN.

HARVEY: We stand shoulder to shoulder.

QUENTIN: We walk alone, one dignified foot in front of the other.

HARVEY: Are you a proud homosexual?

QUENTIN: I call no pigeon hole home.

HARVEY: You believe in gay rights.

QUENTIN: I don't believe that anyone has any rights.

EDWARD: You fought for them.

QUENTIN: I never *fought* for anything.

HARVEY: What were you doing then?

QUENTIN: I was being me.

GERTRUDE laughs and claps her hands together –

GERTRUDE: Amen to that!

QUENTIN: *(To EDWARD.)* I can see you think I've lost my edge, but you see I never had one.

EDWARD: You were a pioneer.

QUENTIN: But I was always pliant. If someone wanted me off a bus, I got off. If someone wanted me to leave their establishment, I left.

EDWARD: But you kept going back, kept getting on the bus –

QUENTIN: I wanted only to be seen to exist. I knew then that society would eventually begin to tolerate me.

HARVEY: I want more than tolerance and acceptance. I want equality.

QUENTIN: One used to hope for the kind of validation that says yes, you are this way but you have worth. You are equal to us, we are equal to you.

EDWARD: Right.

QUENTIN: That's nothing but a pipe dream, a fantasy.

HARVEY: The hell it is!

QUENTIN: We will always be seen to be different, outside the norm. And we will continue to unnerve.

HARVEY: Are you proud?

QUENTIN: Of many things.

HARVEY: But are you proud of being gay?

QUENTIN: I don't care for this line of questioning.

HARVEY: Are you proud to be a homosexual?

QUENTIN: *(To EDWARD.)* Why is it so important to you that I'm proud?

EDWARD: Me?

HARVEY: *(To QUENTIN.)* Jesus. Do you think you're worse than them?

QUENTIN: Worse than whom?

HARVEY: Heterosexuals.

QUENTIN: The world is made for heterosexuals.

GERTRUDE: The world is made for male heterosexuals.

COWBOY appears.

COWBOY: The world is made for white male heterosexuals.

COWBOY disappears.

HARVEY: Do you feel worse than them? Inferior?

QUENTIN: *(To EDWARD.)* Kindly call off your hunting dog.

EDWARD: This isn't my doing.

HARVEY: Do you think you're worse than heterosexuals?

QUENTIN: I accept that I am inadequate.

HARVEY: God damn.

QUENTIN: But I don't think that is part of being gay, I think it is part of being me –

HARVEY: The two are inseparable. They've conditioned you to believe –

QUENTIN: Who's *they?*

HARVEY: Society.

QUENTIN: You're beginning to sound rather paranoid.

HARVEY: And you're delusional.

QUENTIN: I've never pretended to be otherwise.

HARVEY: Are you uncomfortable?

QUENTIN: On this swing? Remarkably so.

HARVEY: With this conversation.

QUENTIN: I should like it to stop now please, yes.

HARVEY: The straight world has made you feel inadequate.

QUENTIN: And which one of us here can say any different?

HARVEY: But that's exactly why I fight it.

GERTRUDE: There are many ways to fight.

QUENTIN points at GERTRUDE.

QUENTIN: She also believes us to be inadequate –

GERTRUDE: I am no cat's mother.

QUENTIN: If Hemingway's book is anything to go by.

GERTRUDE: Hem is full of shit and you sir, are deflecting.

QUENTIN: 'The deed male homosexuals partake in is nasty and repellent and subsequently they are disgusted with themselves. They drink, take drugs and are forever swapping partners in an attempt to mollify this disgust but they cannot ever be really happy.[5]' Isn't that what you said?

GERTRUDE: I was misquoted. It is what he wrote but it is not what I said.

QUENTIN: I'm not saying I think you're wrong.

EDWARD: What? Of course she's wrong.

GERTRUDE: *(Stern.)* I never said it.

QUENTIN: *(To EDWARD.)* Are you seriously suggesting gay men don't take drugs and drink too much?

EDWARD: Some do, yes.

QUENTIN: And is this not to cover their disgust with themselves, their sense of degradation?

EDWARD: For some, maybe.

HARVEY: And for some it's because they happen to like drinking and taking drugs. I never walked away from the meat trucks feeling disgusted or degraded, I felt consummate. Alive.

GERTRUDE: What you do in your beds is your own business and what Alice and I do in ours is not yours.

5   Loosely adapted from *A Moveable Feast* by Ernest Hemingway (1964).

QUENTIN: I think all sex is a mistake.

GERTRUDE: *(To QUENTIN.)* As well as homosexuality itself.

QUENTIN: Now who's deflecting?

GERTRUDE: Foetuses proven to be homosexual ought to be aborted. Or so you told the London Times.

QUENTIN: You shouldn't believe everything you read in the papers.

GERTRUDE: *(Stern.)* Nor what you read in books.

QUENTIN: I see you are all very well versed in my faults.

EDWARD: Did you say that?

QUENTIN: Do not ask me to defend the things that I have said.

HARVEY: Do you believe it?

QUENTIN: The world is a hurtful place, why would anyone choose to be hurt?

HARVEY: What were you doing all those years if you weren't proud?

QUENTIN: *(To EDWARD.)* Why are you hounding me?

EDWARD: I'm not.

QUENTIN: I wanted to make myself visible so that others further down the line wouldn't have to hide.

HARVEY: I'm sad for you.

QUENTIN: I neither crave nor care for your pity.

HARVEY: I think going all those years without feeling proud is pitiable.

QUENTIN: *(Distressed.)* Enough of this.

HARVEY: Are you proud or aren't you?

QUENTIN: *(An outburst.)* What is there to be proud of?

They all look at QUENTIN.

Then slowly they all look out, lost in their own thoughts.

Silence.

There is a ferocious banging and rattling on the central audience door. The sound grows and swells as all the doors in the auditorium begin to shake and rattle.

They look at the doors in fear.

The doors continue to rattle and shake, they reach a crescendo.

The noise stops.

Pause.

QUENTIN: *(Quietly to EDWARD.)* You've loved me since your mother introduced us.

EDWARD: My mum?

QUENTIN: Yes.

EDWARD: *(To himself.)* My mum.

QUENTIN: Yes.

EDWARD holds his chest.

EDWARD: My mum.

QUENTIN: That's right.

EDWARD: She loves anyone that swims against the tide.

Beat.

He looks up at QUENTIN.

She gave me your book. I read it in the park.

QUENTIN: Yes.

EDWARD looks at GERTRUDE.

EDWARD: I read your poetry on the toilet... That carpeting is my landlady's, I'm not sure I'm allowed to change it.

GERTRUDE: *(Perturbed.)* I see.

He looks at HARVEY.

EDWARD: I watched a film about you recently.

HARVEY: *(Flatly.)* Alrighty.

They all look at EDWARD.

EDWARD looks out at the auditorium.

EDWARD: *(Epiphany.)* I'm not Edward.

QUENTIN's swing drops closer to the floor.

QUENTIN: Now we're getting somewhere.

Beat.

EDWARD: What is this? What's happening?

QUENTIN: It would appear your brain is staging some sort of an intervention.

EDWARD: What?

QUENTIN: I thought it obvious.

EDWARD: You still think this is all my doing?

QUENTIN: Unquestionably.

GERTRUDE: Unequivocally.

HARVEY: No doubt about it.

QUENTIN: Your subconscious is trying to get your attention.

EDWARD: I've no idea what you're talking about.

GERTRUDE: *(To herself.)* We're just projections of a mind in flux.

QUENTIN: I imagine we are here only for the length of time it takes for him to figure out what is wrong with him.

EDWARD: *(Repeating, to himself.)* What's wrong with me?

QUENTIN: Then we'll all be whisked away, back to wherever we came from.

GERTRUDE: Back to Alice.

HARVEY: Back to the Castro.

QUENTIN: Back to the great silence.

QUENTIN looks up to the heavens.

Beat.

EDWARD: There's nothing wrong with me.

They all look at him.

GERTRUDE: It's going to be a long night.

HARVEY: *(To EDWARD.)* There must be something you're not seeing, something you're not facing.

GERTRUDE: What is it you can't face?

JULIE ANDREWS dressed as Maria enters. She glares at EDWARD –

JULIE: Tosser.

She disappears back out.

QUENTIN: *(To EDWARD.)* Whatever will you belch up next?

A door swings open. EDWARD ALLEYN enters. He is in his forties and is wearing period doublet and hose.

The door shuts behind him. He leans against it in a louche manner.

ALLEYN: Good even, dear heart.

EDWARD: What?

ALLEYN: Dear heart.

EDWARD: Yes?

ALLEYN: Good even.

EDWARD: … Right.

ALLEYN: God gi' good-e'en.

EDWARD: So sorry?

ALLEYN: God gi' good-e'en?

ALLEYN coughs nervously.

God dig-you-den.

ALLEYN shakes his head in frustration.

God ye good-morrow.

ALLEYN's body twists and contorts as he tries to say the right words.

Good-e'en. Good even. God ye good good. God ye good-morrow. Morrow do you good. Morrow to the day to do you good good. Good to thee, thee and thee and to you all…good times!

He puffs out his cheeks in frustration.

God save us.

He wipes sweat from his brow.

HARVEY: What the hell is this guy saying?

GERTRUDE: I feel I understand him perfectly.

EDWARD: *(To ALLEYN.)* Is everything alright?

ALLEYN holds up his hand.

ALLEYN: Give me leave a sec.

He takes a deep breath, braces himself.

How goes it with thee?

EDWARD: Me?

ALLEYN: Thee. How doth thee do?

ALLEYN shakes his head.

How doth you do?

He hits the back of his own head.

You. Do you do?

He shakes his head, agitated.

How do you –?

EDWARD: Do?

ALLEYN nods enthusiastically, ecstatic with relief.

EDWARD: A little rough actually.

ALLEYN clicks his fingers trying to find the right response –

ALLEYN: Alas… Alack… Ay me?

He shakes his head. Stamps his foot in frustration. He holds his index finger up for pause as he finds the right phrase –

I'm sorry to hear that.

He beams, pleased with himself.

QUENTIN: Is he speaking in tongues?

ALLEYN: Indeed – in the two tongues. Both mine and yours. 'Tis a nightmare. *(To EDWARD.)* I'll warm up in a minute.

He takes a breath.

The venerable Edward Alleyn, tragedian, impresario, lion tamer.

He bows extravagantly.

Did I get it right?

EDWARD: Which bit?

ALLEYN: Any of it. Your modern vernacular hath me in a tight tizzy. 'Tis playing havoc with my senses. I nearly missed my cue back yonder –

He gestures backstage.

He sighs.

My syntax is all o'erthrown.

EDWARD: What are you doing here?

ALLEYN: I sensed a fellow actor in distress.

EDWARD: Who's that then?

ALLEYN: You.

EDWARD: Me?

ALLEYN: You, yes. Or do I hath thee wrong?

EDWARD: An actor.

ALLEYN: Yes, dear heart. For my radar is never off.

HARVEY: *(To EDWARD.)* You're an actor –

EDWARD: I guess that would make sense of the stage and the audience then.

ALLEYN bows extravagantly to the audience.

QUENTIN: You can't be very good.

EDWARD: Pardon?

QUENTIN: You've barely said a word to them.

QUENTIN blows the audience a kiss.

EDWARD picks up his jacket looks at the name written inside, thinks.

EDWARD: … Christopher Marlowe.

ALLEYN: Ah, Kitty.

EDWARD: You knew him?

ALLEYN: Knew him? I was nine-tenths his muse. *(Adopts a different pose for each.)* Faustus, Tamburlaine, The Jew of Malta, Edward II.

EDWARD: Edward II?

ALLEYN: *(Proudly.)* Thou shalt find 'twere I to first portray the troubled sovereign… *(Aside to the audience.)* Possibly.

EDWARD: You were?

ALLEYN: *(Triumphantly.)* I were!

EDWARD: Was.

ALLEYN: What?

EDWARD: Was.

ALLEYN: What was?

EDWARD: You was.

ALLEYN: Was I?

EDWARD: You were.

ALLEYN: When?

EDWARD: When you were Edward II.

ALLEYN: What was I?

EDWARD: You say – I was Edward II.

ALLEYN: *(Excited.)* You were?

EDWARD: No. I wasn't anything –

ALLEYN: *(Sympathetic.)* Oh pooh.

EDWARD: You were Edward II.

ALLEYN: *(Triumphant.)* I were!

HARVEY: May I intervene?

EDWARD: Yes please.

HARVEY: What can you tell us about the role?

ALLEYN: *(Lists off on his hand.)* Troubled King. Terrible judgement. Bit of a whoopsie.

EDWARD: A whoopsie?

ALLEYN: A ganymede.

EDWARD throws him a look.

ALLEYN: Catamite?

EDWARD: Nope.

ALLEYN: Pathic. Cinaedus?

EDWARD: No and no.

ALLEYN: Bugger.

EDWARD: Really?

ALLEYN: Sodomite.

EDWARD: Worse.

ALLEYN: Brother to a brother?

EDWARD: I don't think so.

ALLEYN: A homosexual.

EDWARD: Thank you.

ALLEYN: Except he wasn't.

EDWARD: Wasn't what?

ALLEYN: A homosexual. For 'tis your terminology and not our own, nor was't his. We're not big on labels.

QUENTIN: *(A point proven.)* Aha!

EDWARD: What about the ones you just listed?

ALLEYN: They cover a wide range of sin. Sodomite can mean anything from laying with a prostitute to fiddling a chicken.

HARVEY: But this King Edward –

ALLEYN: In love with another man, indeed. But, look you, labelling him thus would be to miss the point.

EDWARD: What point?

ALLEYN: We're all the same. What is more, everything is within us – all possibilities of experience and sin. We are all but one temptation away from murdering, stealing or buggering thy neighbour.

QUENTIN: Heavens to Betsy!

GERTRUDE: Sexuality is a continuum.

ALLEYN: Homosexuality is a mortal sin. It is testament to the strength of one's moral servitude how well one is able to bat back these human urges.

HARVEY: *(Proudly.)* Then I am weak as a kitten.

ALLEYN: O 'tis easy done to be sure. Our penchant for bed sharing has laid low many a noble mind. Cooks with serving maids, scholars with students, travellers on a budget. A hapless stretch in the dark, a grappling of hands after some night terror, a tussle too far for the bedcloths. Farm hands retiring after a long day of shucking corn, *(He moves unconsciously to the front of the stage, beginning to get lost in his vision.)* snuggle for warmth and awake to find themselves, after a turn too far in the night, nose to nose. The one breathing warm breath softly in t'other's ear, their strong limbs entwined, their eyes meet as the cock riseth for its morning croak...

He looks skittishly at the others, composes himself.

Be it concluded, all sin is within the heart of every man.

EDWARD: Gotcha.

ALLEYN: Know't I have ne'er transgressed myself.

QUENTIN: *(Sardonic.)* You must be very strong.

ALLEYN: I have eyes only for my wife.

GERTRUDE: Lucky her.

ALLEYN: In few, I am yet to spend my seed in another's thatch.

EDWARD turns round to GERTRUDE –

EDWARD: I'm an actor.

GERTRUDE: *(With distaste.)* I heard.

EDWARD: You help artists.

GERTRUDE: I do. I have.

EDWARD: Well – I'm an artist.

GERTRUDE pulls an uncomfortable face.

EDWARD: What? Actors are artists.

GERTRUDE makes a noise of uncertainty.

EDWARD: Oh *come on.*

GERTRUDE: Young man, I have only now just learned that I am some awful imitation of myself dreamt up by you and presented on a toilet. What on earth makes you think I can help anyone?

EDWARD: You're Gertrude Stein. You've nurtured many a talent – Matisse, Picasso, Thornton Wilder –

GERTRUDE: Talent being the operative word.

HARVEY: We all want to get out of here right?

QUENTIN: I never knew how much I'd taken gravity for granted.

GERTRUDE: In a horrible twist of irony I do find myself desperate for the loo.

They all look to GERTRUDE.

GERTRUDE sighs.

GERTRUDE: Clearly Edward II is of some import.

EDWARD: Agreed.   HARVEY: Agreed.   QUENTIN: Agreed.

EDWARD holds up his jacket.

EDWARD: I figure this must be some sort of costume.

HARVEY: Thatta boy Eddie!

QUENTIN: *(Epiphany.)* You were playing the part of
Edward II.

ALLEYN: Dear heart! I'm sure you were wonderful.

GERTRUDE: I'd endeavour to suggest there is something
in the role that has struck a chord. Something that has
triggered a deep reaction within you.

HARVEY: Let's find that trigger Eddie!

EDWARD: Absolutely.

Beat.

EDWARD is a blank.

EDWARD: How do I do that then?

GERTRUDE: Find the golden thread.

*He begins looking around the space. Catches himself and looks back
at GERTRUDE.*

GERTRUDE: It is not a literal thread, but if you are any kind of
an artist it will be palpable. Every artist is indelibly linked
to his work by a golden thread, connecting the creator
to their creations. Pablo used to say he could feel them
tied to his knuckles, his earlobes, his ankles, his teeth. He
could sense the pull of his pieces wherever they were in
the world. Find your thread, the thing that drew you to
Edward and Edward to you, the thing that connects your
consciousness with his, and then we will find the kink, the
place where the line has gotten twisted, the tangle that has
landed you here.

Beat.

HARVEY: Golly Gert, you're good at this.

GERTRUDE: What drew you to the part?

EDWARD is a blank.

What choices did you make as an artist?

Beat.

EDWARD puts his head in his hands.

EDWARD: Maybe actors aren't artists.

HARVEY: Hey, Alleyn.

ALLEYN: Say you?

HARVEY: What choices did you make with Edward II?

ALLEYN: O, a frown – troubled. A sloping shoulder – in disgrace. A sickly pallor – lovelorn. And a rouge shoe – fancy.

EDWARD: What was your process?

ALLEYN: Through the double doors on a sweeping arc to the left.

EDWARD: What psychological choices did you make?

ALLEYN looks at him blankly.

EDWARD: What did you ask Marlowe about the role?

ALLEYN: What is my cue and what am I holding?

EDWARD slowly head-butts the back of the stage.

QUENTIN: Mr Alleyn.

ALLEYN: Signor!

QUENTIN: We believe our friend here has gotten himself confused.

ALLEYN: Alas.

QUENTIN: In playing the role of Edward II, we think he may have muddled himself with the character and landed in a pickle.

ALLEYN: That happened to a friend of mine.

EDWARD: It did?

ALLEYN: For a fortnight he thought himself Beelzebub.

EDWARD: A fortnight! Then what happened?

ALLEYN: He set himself alight and threw himself in the Thames.

EDWARD: Right.

ALLEYN: But – it also happened to my wife's brother's neighbour.

EDWARD: Okay.

ALLEYN: She awaked one morn to thinking herself a carrot.

EDWARD: And what happened to her?

ALLEYN: They took her for a mind diseased, locked her up in the asylum and threw away the key.

EDWARD: Not fantastically reassuring either.

QUENTIN: *(To EDWARD.)* Is it not the modern actor's way to draw on their own life? To scour their emotional landscape, to use their past hurts to inform and fuel their work?

EDWARD: If you say so.

ALLEYN: Whatever for?

QUENTIN: To enrich the inner life of their character, or so they'll tell you.

HARVEY: Sounds a lot like free therapy to me.

GERTRUDE: Drama as therapy – there's nothing worse.

All except EDWARD, look out at the audience and grimace awkwardly.

ALLEYN: There are only five questions that need asking in the theatre – are the audience crying? Are they laughing? How much are they crying? How much are they laughing? And what is my return on the box office?

GERTRUDE: *(To EDWARD.)* What emotional pain did you draw on?

A door swings open. GAVESTON enters in Elizabethan doublet and hose. He is a similar age to EDWARD. The door swings shut behind him.

EDWARD: Gaveston! My Gaveston.

GAVESTON: … No.

ALLEYN: *(Aside to audience.)* Awkward.

EDWARD: I'm so sorry I thought you were someone else.

GAVESTON: I am Gaveston.

EDWARD: Okay –

GAVESTON: And I'm also not him.

EDWARD is confused.

GAVESTON: It seems I'm a little bit him and a little bit someone else.

EDWARD: Which bit of him is you?

GAVESTON: Hard to tell.

EDWARD: And who's the other bit?

GAVESTON: You know who I am.

EDWARD: I haven't a clue. Give us a clue.

GAVESTON: Billy.

EDWARD: Billy.

GAVESTON: Yeah.

EDWARD: Billy is my clue.

GAVESTON: Billy is my name.

Beat.

A penny drops.

EDWARD: Shit.

GAVESTON: Thanks.

EDWARD: Sorry.

GAVESTON: It's okay.

EDWARD: Not – you are shit

GAVESTON: Sure.

EDWARD: Shit generally.

GAVESTON: I see.

EDWARD: Universal shit.

HARVEY: *(To EDWARD.)* Breathe.

EDWARD: What? Yes. Breathe.

He takes a deep breath in and out.

GAVESTON: How've you been?

EDWARD: A bit confused.

GAVESTON: I can see that. What have you got me wearing?

EDWARD: Me? Oh right yes – it's a doublet and hose.

GAVESTON: Doublet and who?

EDWARD: It doesn't matter. *(Sincere.)* You look great.

They take each other in.

Beat.

EDWARD tries to break the tension –

EDWARD: You seen all this then?

He gestures to the theatre.

GAVESTON moves downstage, taking it all in.

EDWARD moves with him. It's as if they're now in their own space, unable to hear the others who are watching attentively.

GAVESTON: *(Intrigued.)* This is your psyche.

EDWARD: Oh right.

He looks to the others for confirmation.

Is it?

The others nod.

It is.

GAVESTON: Candlelit and carved in oak.

EDWARD: Yes, wow.

GAVESTON: Fancy. It's a bit crowded.

EDWARD: It is. But still, I'm quite impressed with myself –
who knew I had such a beautiful psyche?

GERTRUDE rolls her eyes.

GERTRUDE: Actors really are the worst narcissists.

HARVEY: Shhh.

*HARVEY, GERTRUDE and QUENTIN lean in, they watch EDWARD
and GAVESTON fondly. HARVEY eats his popcorn, transfixed.*

EDWARD: You look good.

GAVESTON: You said.

EDWARD: Yes, sorry.

GAVESTON: I've not seen you since –

EDWARD: No. *(Softly.)*
Not Hylas was more mourned of Hercules
Than thou hast been of me since thy exile.[6]

GAVESTON: I've missed you too.

EDWARD and GAVESTON smile affectionately at each other.

EDWARD: You're like them. *(The others.)* Both here and not here?

GAVESTON: I think so.

GERTRUDE: *(Sorrowful.)* I am nothing but the memory of others.

---

6   From *Edward II* by Christopher Marlowe (1594).

EDWARD: So I can say what I want?

GAVESTON: Give it a try.

EDWARD: *Wanker.*

GAVESTON: How'd it feel?

EDWARD: Pretty good.

HARVEY: *(To QUENTIN.)* Did you find love, Quentin?

QUENTIN: No, there is no tall, dark man waiting for me up there. *(He looks up at the ceiling.)* It's an odd thing really, to think we've been here for years, that we'll be here for years to come and still there will be no one to call my own.

GAVESTON: *(To EDWARD.)* What did you want to say to me?

HARVEY: *(To QUENTIN.)* I'm sorry to hear that.

EDWARD: *(To GAVESTON.)* I haven't the faintest.

QUENTIN: *(To HARVEY.)* Don't be. I've had happy times of course, but I've long since learned to rely solely on myself.

GAVESTON: I haven't seen you since we were in that pub. The one off the Strand –

EDWARD: The Nell Gwynne, it's got that brilliant jukebox.

QUENTIN: *(Mostly to himself.)* It's not that I was undesirous of it, you understand, I suppose I just never thought it was a possibility for me.

GAVESTON: I haven't thought about that place in years.

EDWARD: You broke up with me in that pub.

QUENTIN: I was always happy just to settle for a little kindness.

EDWARD: You said it wasn't working.

GAVESTON: I did. It wasn't.

EDWARD: And then you left.

GAVESTON nods.

Beat.

EDWARD: I went on a trip to Berkley Castle, after we split up –
I got the train there, on my own. It's in Gloucestershire. I
needed fresh air, countryside. I needed to unhook myself
from you. I was seeing you in everything – cafes we'd been
to, cinemas, films we'd seen, I even saw you in condiments
– which ones you liked, which you didn't. I needed to
tread out some new ground, gather some new experiences,
see things that weren't about you. But of course, I thought
about you the whole way there. You were in the trees,
the sandwiches, on the empty seat next to me. It's where
Edward II was kept – Berkley Castle – imprisoned. They've
still got the dungeon, you can see it – go up to it, look down
it. It's about forty foot deep and only about six foot wide.
They reckon he might've been there for weeks. Stood there
alone, shivering in the shit. I remember looking down
it, this deep black hole and thinking – this is where love
gets you.

ALLEYN: *(Softly.)* My mind's distempered, and my body's numbed,
And whether I have limbs or no I know not.
O, would my blood dropp'd out from ev'ry vein,
As doth this water from my tattered robes.[7]

GAVESTON: If I was here, I'd tell you that it had to happen.

QUENTIN: They did an experiment on rats. They isolated
them, removed them from their pack. Left them alone in
cages and measured the effect on their amygdala –

GAVESTON: *(To EDWARD.)* That it was right that it happened.

---

7   From *Edward II* by Christopher Marlowe (1594).

QUENTIN: It's an almond-shaped part of the brain that regulates emotions, survival instinct, memory. It swells under stress or fear.

GAVESTON: *(To EDWARD.)* If I was here, I'd tell you that I'm sorry.

QUENTIN: They found that the amygdala swelled in the brain of the isolated rat. It didn't shrink back down even when it was put back in with its pack. The poor creature carried its trauma with it.

GAVESTON: And if I was here, I'd tell you that I did love you.

EDWARD looks at GAVESTON.

Blood begins to seep out of HARVEY's chest staining and spreading across his shirt. He looks down and notices it.

The others all turn to look at him.

HARVEY touches the bloody patch and inspects his fingers.

The others step toward him. HARVEY holds up a firm hand to stop them.

The others take another step toward him. HARVEY holds up his other hand firmly stopping them in their tracks. He shakes his head at them.

With great dignity HARVEY slowly puts his jacket back on, covering the patch. He buttons his jacket and nods reassuringly at the others.

A hatch in the front of the stage opens, THATCHER tumbles out in a military tuck-and-roll. She's lost her scarf and jacket, her shirt is untucked. She stands up, brushes herself down.

EDWARD: *(To THATCHER.)* No. Not now. Not you – out.

He points for her to leave.

THATCHER, disappointed, looks at him imploringly.

EDWARD: I mean it. I don't want you in here.

THATCHER's disappointment turns to rage.

She points at EDWARD.

THATCHER: Shame!

She begins backing out toward an exit.

Shame!

She takes off a high-heel and throws at him.

Shame!

Glitter cannons explode across the space.

THATCHER exits.

The characters stand motionless.

The glitter settles.

GAVESTON: Was she cursing you?

QUENTIN: She was trying to help.

EDWARD looks at QUENTIN.

The hatch in the ceiling opens, sheets of newspaper fall through. Lots of them. They cover the stage.

He picks up a paper – it's a copy of The Sun.

He reads aloud from it –

EDWARD: '"I'd shoot my son if he had AIDS," says vicar. 7th February 1985.'

He picks up another paper –

'December 1987. In response to the firebombing of the London offices of newspaper Capital Gay, Tory MP Elaine

Kellet-Bowman exclaimed "quite right too" in the House of Commons.'

GERTRUDE stands abruptly, she looks around vacantly, confused.

GERTRUDE: Where's Alice?

EDWARD: 'She refused to condemn the bombing, arguing that she was "quite prepared to affirm that there should be an intolerance of evil."'

GERTRUDE: Where's my Alice?

She begins to move absentmindedly about the space.

EDWARD picks up another paper, becoming frantic now –

EDWARD: '"I would put 90% of queers in the ruddy gas chambers," says Bill Brownhill, Tory leader of South Staffordshire Council.'

QUENTIN looks up at the heavens.

QUENTIN: *(Speaking in Polari.)* In the beginning, Gloria created the heaven and the earth.[8]

EDWARD picks up another paper.

EDWARD: 'Burning is too good for them.'

QUENTIN: And the earth was nanti form, and void; and munge was upon the eke of the deep.

GERTRUDE: Is she coming?

She begins slowly waltzing around the space.

EDWARD: 'Bury them in a pit and pour on quick lime.'

QUENTIN: And the Fairy of Gloria trolled upon the eke of the aqua.

---

8   QUENTIN's lines in this section have been taken from polaribible.org.

HARVEY stands, he covers his eyes with his hands.

HARVEY: I walked among the angry and sad gay sisters and brothers last night at City Hall and late last night as they lit candles[9] –

QUENTIN: And Gloria cackled, Let there be sparkle: and there was sparkle.

HARVEY: They stood in silence on Castro Street reaching out for some symbolic thing that would give them hope…

EDWARD continues to rifle through the papers –

EDWARD: 'Daily Mail, 1993 – Abortion hope after "gay gene" finding.'

He picks up another paper.

'All homosexuals should be exterminated to stop the spread of AIDS.'

In a frenzy EDWARD goes through the papers, he reads a section then throws them across the stage –

COWBOY appears and softly sings the opening bars to an eighties gay anthem.

HARVEY: These were strong people…people whose faces I knew, and people whom I never saw before, but who I knew. They were strong and even they needed hope –

EDWARD reads a word from each newspaper then discards it –

EDWARD: 'Perverts.' 'Benders.' 'Degenerates.'

The LEATHER MAN, JUDY GARLAND and JULIE ANDREWS appear. They and QUENTIN softly back COWBOY's song.

The singers hum gently under the following, the effect is beautiful.

GERTRUDE's waltzing is becoming manic.

---

9   From Harvey Milk's 'The Hope Speech' (1978).

ALLEYN delivers his lines simply and with a deep emotional connection.

ALLEYN: The mightiest Kings have had their minions.

EDWARD: 'Paedophiles.' 'Diseased.' 'Filthy.'

HARVEY: And those young gays who are 'coming out'– to them the only thing that they have to look forward to is hope…

GAVESTON: *(To EDWARD.)* You used to be so worried about your body.

EDWARD: 'Remove them.' 'Hang them.'

GAVESTON: *(To EDWARD.)* And you worried that you smelled. You'd constantly ask me if you smelled bad.

EDWARD: 'Castrate them.' 'Gas them.'

GAVESTON: Like you thought there was something rotten inside you, like you were scared it had started to seep out, show itself.

HARVEY: And *you* have to give them hope.

EDWARD fights with the papers, kicking and throwing them violently across the stage.

HARVEY: Hope for a better world.

EDWARD collapses in a heap at the front of the stage, his head in his hands.

HARVEY: Hope for a better tomorrow.

GAVESTON: *(To EDWARD.)* I did love you.

EDWARD pulls his jacket over his head.

ALLEYN: Great Alexander loved Hephaestion.

HARVEY: Hope for a place to go to if the pressures at home are too great. Hope that all will be alright.

ALLEYN: And for Patroclus stern Achilles droop'd.

GERTRUDE is now wildly spinning around the space.

HARVEY: Without hope, not only the gays but the blacks, the seniors, the poor, the handicaps the *us*-es give up.

HARVEY removes his hands from his eyes. He passionately addresses the audience –

HARVEY: If I get elected it will mean that a green light is lit – a green light that says to all who feel lost and disenfranchised that you now can go forward – it means hope and we – no, you and you and you and yes you got to give them hope.

The central doors swing open.

The singing stops.

MARGARET THATCHER enters, deeply dishevelled. Her mascara has run down her face, her hair is a mess and she is hobbling on her one high heel.

The LEATHER MAN, the COWBOY, JULIE and JUDY exit.

GERTRUDE stops waltzing.

THATCHER takes in the room. She's out of breath, exhausted, but energised by a need to say something.

She takes in a deep breath and with great determination she sings Gloria Gaynor's 'I Am What I Am' a cappella. It's a strange but wilful performance, she's not a singer and her desperation makes her voice shaky. She sings through gritted teeth.

EDWARD removes the jacket from his head and watches, bewildered.

THATCHER takes off her high heel and begins a strange half-hearted tap routine. She shuffles uncertainly in a circle.

The others stare on agog.

At the end of the song, THATCHER backs into the doorway and raises her arms for applause as the doors slam shut on her.

Beat.

EDWARD: Shame.

QUENTIN: Quite.

EDWARD: No – *shame.*

EDWARD stands.

HARVEY: That's what the broad shouted at you.

GAVESTON: When she cursed you –

QUENTIN: She wasn't cursing anyone.

EDWARD: In a way she was… She did.

QUENTIN: I'm afraid you've lost me.

EDWARD: Her Government… They… She – validated homophobia.

QUENTIN: I think that's overstating it.

EDWARD: She made it illegal for teachers to talk to the gay kids about how they were feeling.

QUENTIN: We've all had to bear much worse.

EDWARD: I grew up thinking that there was something wrong with me, something so wrong that it couldn't be talked about – –so yeah, in a way she did curse me. She cursed a whole generation.

QUENTIN: May I remind you that that wasn't the Lady herself, that was your subconscious disguised as her. I can't imagine the real Maggie went in a great deal for tap dancing.

GERTRUDE: Or singing by the sounds of it.

EDWARD: That's why I'm here… I saw shame in Edward the Second and he brought out the shame in me.

QUENTIN's swing drops to the floor.

QUENTIN: Hallelujah!

HARVEY: Thatta boy Eddie!

QUENTIN steps off the swing and kisses the floor.

GERTRUDE tries a door – it's still locked.

GERTRUDE: We're not out of the woods yet.

EDWARD: *(To GERTRUDE.)* Shame is the golden thread. Shame is the thing that led me to Edward.

ALLEYN: 'Twas ten shillings a week that led me to him.

EDWARD: Right, well that's valid too.

QUENTIN: We were birthed in shame. When they christened us they cursed us. 'Homosexuals.'

HARVEY: They coined the term to shame us, control us.

QUENTIN: We were thought such a threat to the social structure.

HARVEY: And some of us are. Joyously so!

ALLEYN: The same was said of actors once. *(To EDWARD.)* Dear heart, they were terrified of us in the provinces.

QUENTIN: *(Sorrowful.)* As though the very fabric of society would be ripped asunder if we were allowed to love and live freely.

EDWARD: *(To himself.)* All we are is everything everyone has ever said to us.

GERTRUDE: *(Disdainfully.)* That is why one is usually more mindful of the company one keeps.

EDWARD: So if our environment, our society tells us we're inferior, abnormal – what are you meant to do with that?

QUENTIN: Bury the sadness deep within yourself and keep walking.

GERTRUDE: Endeavour to reduce one's environment to fit one's needs.

HARVEY: Shout from the rooftops and keep shouting until things change.

GERTRUDE: We've always unnerved the patriarchy.

HARVEY: In a hyper-masculinised society, male homosexuality is the ultimate sin.

GERTRUDE: My dear, lesbians have fared little better – they feared us before they even accepted we existed.

GAVESTON: Try being black and gay.

COWBOY pops his head around a door.

COWBOY: Preach Sister!

He disappears again.

ALLEYN clears his throat and steps forward.

ALLEYN: As the only male on the stage who lays himself with females, methinks 'tis incumbent upon me to suggest, nay – insist that 'tis hard for us too. Living up to the male ideal is an impossible and cruel task that has been thrust upon us.

He politely steps back.

GAVESTON sits away from the others, slowly goes through the papers scattered on the floor.

EDWARD: *(To himself.)* You're not worthy of love.

GERTRUDE: Who isn't?

EDWARD: It's what Canterbury said.

QUENTIN: Who is Canterbury?

EDWARD: He was here.

QUENTIN: When?

EDWARD: Earlier. Except of course, he wasn't.

QUENTIN: He wasn't?

EDWARD: If you are me, then he was me.

QUENTIN: Who is whom?

GERTRUDE: *(To QUENTIN.)* If you are he and I am he and we are he, then he that was here earlier was also he, when he was here.

QUENTIN: *(Exasperated.)* God love you Gertrude but I do wish you'd learn to speak plainly!

EDWARD: If you're all figments of my sub-conscious then really I'm talking to myself.

QUENTIN: How indulgent.

GERTRUDE: Certainly we cannot consider this an objective exercise.

HARVEY: He said you weren't worthy of love?

EDWARD: Yes, except that was me saying that.

QUENTIN: To whom?

EDWARD: To me.

QUENTIN: I think I was better off on the swing, I seem to have lost perspective.

HARVEY: Do you think you are worthy of it?

EDWARD: Love? Isn't everybody?

QUENTIN: Don't ask me, I'm on the verge of a turn. I think it's the change in altitude.

GERTRUDE: *(To EDWARD.)* Yes, but it's a different thing to know it.

EDWARD: Right. Then I don't.

HARVEY: You don't think you are, or you don't know that you are?

EDWARD: I've confused myself.

QUENTIN: You've confused us all.

GERTRUDE: It's simple.

HARVEY: Dish it, Gert.

GERTRUDE: You felt at school that you were different. You were told you didn't belong.

EDWARD: Yeah I was badly bullied.

GERTRUDE: This awareness that you didn't fit made your young mind tell itself that there must be something wrong with you. Something flawed. This feeling of being inherently flawed is your shame. It has been with you your whole life. It has grown and it has collected evidence to support itself. It has gathered momentum and led you to this point. This point, where, before a room full of strangers, you are telling yourself you are not worthy of love.

QUENTIN: It's quite the headache.

HARVEY: Nicely served, Gerty.

QUENTIN: *(To HARVEY.)* Why aren't you telling him off for not being proud?

EDWARD: I am proud of being gay.

HARVEY: As you should be!

QUENTIN: My head's in a flat spin.

GERTRUDE: *(To EDWARD.)* Even though you've come to terms with your homosexuality you're still dealing with the fallout of having believed your whole life that you were inherently flawed. It has informed everything. Every impulse, choice, every interaction you've had, has come from this – this broken place deep within your self. This shame.

Beat.

EDWARD nods.

GERTRUDE: It has informed *everything* –

She cocks her head toward GAVESTON.

EDWARD doesn't get what she's doing.

She winks at EDWARD and cocks her head again toward GAVESTON.

EDWARD: *(To GERTRUDE.)* You alright?

QUENTIN: *(Exasperated.)* May the good Lord preserve us.

HARVEY: *(To GAVESTON.)* Hey Gav – whatcha reading?

GAVESTON looks up from the papers.

QUENTIN shoves EDWARD towards him.

GAVESTON: *(To EDWARD.)* These are all from the Eighties and early Nineties.

EDWARD: I guess that would make sense.

GAVESTON: Shitty time to be gay in Britain. Little kids soaking all this up. With nothing else to measure ourselves by.

GAVESTON tosses the papers to the side.

EDWARD smiles softly at him.

GAVESTON: No wonder you were bullied.

EDWARD: They were soaking all this up too.

Beat.

GAVESTON: We didn't stand much of a chance together did we?

EDWARD shakes his head sadly.

GAVESTON: You drew on the pain of our break-up to understand Edward and Gaveston.

Small beat.

EDWARD: I drew on the love too.

ALLEYN clears his throat loudly.

ALLEYN: Couldn't you just say the lines?

EDWARD: What?

ALLEYN: Proclaim them as they are writ, rather than all this conjuring of past whatsits. Burbage used to babble on about such practices but I'faith methinks one runs the risk of over-basting the bird.

QUENTIN: It's certainly sent this one *(EDWARD.)* up the creek.

ALLEYN: And if I may –

QUENTIN: Indeed you may.

ALLEYN: *(To EDWARD.)* Edward the Second knew not your shame.

HARVEY: Says who?

ALLEYN: All sin is in the heart of every fallen man. Who he is, we all are. Therefore he won't have felt shame for his person.

HARVEY: He can't have been feeling very good about himself.

ALLEYN: I warrant you, the shame of his fallen reign would've burnt brightly for him. So too, that his will was weaker than his urges. In essence – shame for his actions, but not of himself. And actions do not maketh the man.

QUENTIN: You have a fluid notion of identity.

ALLEYN: Indeed, we judge the sin but not the sinner.

QUENTIN: It's what I've been arguing all along – there's no need to categorise and label any of us.

ALLEYN: *(To EDWARD.)* It is not what Kitty writ.

EDWARD: No, because he didn't have the terminology for it. I get that this sort of shame is a modern concept, but I look at Edward as a gay man and I see shame in him.

ALLEYN: Shame for his actions –

EDWARD: *(Impassioned.)* Shame for who he is, shame in his core, his being. He's spent his whole life recognising that he isn't like his dad, his brother, the men he's surrounded by, that he isn't a 'real boy.' His environment told him that his impulses were wrong, invalid, and he grew up certain in the knowledge that somewhere deep down inside himself, in the base pit of his being, there was something foul and rotting. All the while he's being prepped to be his father, literally told by divine law that his purpose, his reason for being, is to become the man his dad is. Live up to his ideal. Wear his crown. So he suppresses himself, he pushes who he is deep within himself and tries to conform, to please, to gain the validation that he has never felt. He tries to drown out this voice that says he isn't good enough, that he isn't worthy enough. He throws extravagant parties, flamboyantly throws his riches around to compensate for it. He desperately tries to cover this stinking stagnant well within him with glitz and sequins and fine wines and banquets. But all that he has tried to suppress begins to explode and he can no longer bolster the dam.

GERTRUDE: *(Softly.)* Good boy.

GAVESTON: *(To EDWARD.)* But he has love.

EDWARD: For a time.

GAVESTON: A short, but beautiful time.

EDWARD smiles at GAVESTON.

EDWARD: But it's more than love, it's obsessional love. He found in you –

GAVESTON: In Gaveston.

EDWARD: Someone whom he could hide behind. Someone braver, louder, funnier than he was. Someone whom he could hide his shame behind. Someone whose shadow I could grow in.

GAVESTON: You?

EDWARD: Me. Yes. Us. Edward and I both. We hid behind you Billy and Gaveston. I used you to cover up how shit I felt about myself. It's why it hurt so much when you left, because when you left you didn't just take your love, you took away the buffer, the barrier to my shame.

Beat.

GAVESTON: I did love you.

EDWARD: And I loved you.

GAVESTON: It broke.

EDWARD: It did.

He kisses GAVESTON tenderly on his forehead.

Wherever you are, I hope you're happy.

GAVESTON blows out some of the candles and leaves, the door shuts behind him.

ALLEYN steps forward.

ALLEYN: Things are better for your kind today?

EDWARD: They are better.

HARVEY: They're not equal.

EDWARD: But they're better.

GERTRUDE: There's been progression but no completion.

QUENTIN: It's still not safe.

EDWARD: *(To QUENTIN.)* More safe than you were. But no, not safe. Not entirely.

ALLEYN: But things have improved?

EDWARD: Here, they have.

HARVEY: All over the world we're having to flee our homes.

GERTRUDE: We're being hung beaten stoned.

QUENTIN: We're being imprisoned or pushed off buildings strapped to chairs.

EDWARD: But where I live, yes I'm lucky, I can stand here in public *(He looks out at the audience.)* and say I'm gay.

There is a loud knocking and rattling on all the doors in the auditorium.

They look out nervously.

The noise begins to decrease and diminish until eventually there is just a knocking coming from the central audience doors.

It stops.

GERTRUDE: Something still wants in.

ALLEYN blows out some of the candles and leaves. The door shuts behind him.

The knocking returns on the central audience doors.

The others huddle close together as the banging continues.

The banging stops.

They remain huddled, nervous and focused on the door.

EDWARD: Things are better now.

QUENTIN: But they're not safe.

HARVEY: Not entirely.

EDWARD: No, not entirely.

GERTRUDE: There is no safety in the safeness.

QUENTIN: One must never take it for granted.

HARVEY: We gotta keep watch.

QUENTIN: Remain vigilant.

GERTRUDE: We must keep ourselves robust.

HARVEY: Despite all our hard work there is still something.

QUENTIN: Something.

GERTRUDE: Something eating away at us.

QUENTIN: A termite silently burrowing.

GERTRUDE: We must fix ourselves.

HARVEY: Collectively.

EDWARD: From the inside.

HARVEY: There's time now.

QUENTIN: There was no room for introspection before.

GERTRUDE: We were too busy trying to survive.

QUENTIN: … Beaten.

GERTRUDE: Forced into hiding.

HARVEY: Murdered.

> *HARVEY touches the bloody patch under his jacket.*
>
> *They all turn to look at him.*
>
> *Beat.*
>
> *There is a loud knocking and rattling on the central audience doors.*
>
> *They huddle closer together.*
>
> *The knocking stops.*

GERTRUDE: Who is it?

EDWARD: Shhhh!

HARVEY: It sounds angry.

EDWARD: It's shame.

QUENTIN: Yes.   HARVEY: Yes.   GERTRUDE: Yes.

QUENTIN: But in what form?

GERTRUDE: What shape?

HARVEY: The cops.

QUENTIN: The roughs.

GERTRUDE: My brother.

EDWARD: No, it's mine. It belongs to me.

QUENTIN: Yes.   HARVEY: Yes.   GERTRUDE: Yes.

HARVEY: It's someone big.

QUENTIN: The one whom you're most afraid of.

GERTRUDE: Who first told you you were flawed?

HARVEY: Who was it that first said it was a bad thing to be as
   you are?

EDWARD: Lots of people. I was bullied, like I said.

QUENTIN: There was a ringleader.

EDWARD: Yes.   HARVEY: Yes.   GERTRUDE: Yes.

QUENTIN: One you feared the most.

EDWARD: Yes.   HARVEY: Yes.   GERTRUDE: Yes.

QUENTIN: Let's call him Errol.

EDWARD: Well that was his name.

QUENTIN: That's why I said let's call him Errol.

EDWARD: Errol.   HARVEY: Errol.   GERTRUDE: Errol.

EDWARD, HARVEY and GERTRUDE begin to move as one, a chorus.

ALL: *(But QUENTIN.)* Do you think it's him?

QUENTIN: There's only one way to find out.

They look towards the central audience doors.

A fierce knocking comes from it.

QUENTIN joins the chorus.

They're terrified.

ALL: Oh, God.

Another fierce knocking.

ALL: Oh, shit.

They cover their faces.

ALL: Come in?

Beat.

The central audience doors fly open and ERROL storms in. He's a seven-year-old boy with a school backpack on. He's carrying a lit candle.

He walks with fierce determination toward EDWARD, cursing him in his cockney accent as he does –

ERROL: Poof!

Poofter!

Bender!

Shirt-lifter!

Faggot!

EDWARD opens his eyes and sees that ERROL is just a little boy.

EDWARD: ... Oh.

The others continue to cower behind EDWARD.

ERROL: Batty-boy!

Gaylord!

EDWARD: ... Any others?

ERROL scratches his head.

ERROL: Bum-bandit.

EDWARD: Well remembered.

ERROL studies EDWARD.

ERROL: You got old.

EDWARD: ...Thank you.

ERROL: You're well scared of me.

EDWARD: I'm not sure that's –

ERROL makes a menacing step toward him.

EDWARD, and the others behind him, flinch.

EDWARD: Okay well, maybe marginally.

ERROL: It's not me you should be scared of.

EDWARD: Okay.

ERROL: You need to own that this is all a self-construct.

EDWARD: ... Right.

ERROL: Perpetuated only by you.

EDWARD: … Okay.

ERROL: Look there were some unfortunate socio-political circumstances when you were growing up that made you feel unworthy, invalid, that much is true. There were also individuals who then went on to exacerbate those feelings of inadequacy. But it is you that continues to fan the flames. It is your own belief in your own deficiencies that keeps the negativity burning.

EDWARD: You're very articulate.

ERROL beams, pleased with himself.

EDWARD: I don't remember you being this articulate.

ERROL: I wasn't. I'm not. The real Errol is out there somewhere living his life.

EDWARD: What do you think he's doing?

ERROL: Something brilliant… He's probably an astronaut.

EDWARD: Wicked.

Beat. ERROL takes EDWARD in.

ERROL: I'm sorry I bullied you. But you've got to stop rolling me out every time you wanna feel bad about yourself. It's exhausting.

EDWARD: Sorry.

ERROL takes off his rucksack and holds it up for EDWARD.

ERROL: For you.

EDWARD steps away from the others and takes the bag.

He looks at it.

EDWARD: It's my schoolbag.

ERROL: It's got Dungeons and Dragons on the front, you used to like that.

EDWARD: Yeah, I did. Though if I was able to have been honest, it would've had Kylie on the front. I liked her more.

He smiles at ERROL.

Perhaps if I was at school now, I could have.

ERROL shrugs.

ERROL: Perhaps.

He contemplates EDWARD.

Laters, loser.

EDWARD: Laters.

ERROL leaves via the central audience doors.

EDWARD sits on the lip of the stage and contemplates the bag.

The others look at each other.

They rouse themselves and separate.

They slowly begin to clear up the stage behind EDWARD.

They collect the newspapers and pile them neatly.

GERTRUDE and HARVEY gently begin outing the remaining candles.

There is a slight solemn mood amongst them as they work, a sense that they are shutting things down.

QUENTIN picks up EDWARD's jacket, holds it up and inspects it.

QUENTIN: Poor Edward. At the bottom of his pit.

GERTRUDE: Do you think he knew there were better days coming?

HARVEY: Not for him.

QUENTIN: No, indeed. Not for him.

EDWARD turns to look at them.

EDWARD: I think he thought about legacy.

HARVEY: His own?

EDWARD: The one he was joining, stepping into. All those who had gone before him. The long line of mighty Kings and Queens who have passed. I think he called on them for strength.

QUENTIN, HARVEY and GERTRUDE stop what they're doing and survey the audience.

They speak softly to each other –

GERTRUDE: Are we remembered?

HARVEY: Honoured?

QUENTIN: Loved?

Pause.

GERTRUDE: *(To QUENTIN.)* Alice isn't coming, is she?

QUENTIN shakes his head no.

HARVEY: And they're not waiting for me at the Castro are they?

QUENTIN shakes his head, no.

GERTRUDE outs the final candles – leaving only one candelabra still lit.

EDWARD turns to look at her.

She nods at him, he nods back.

She smiles sadly.

They both look at HARVEY who winks at EDWARD. EDWARD nods back.

HARVEY sighs resignedly.

GERTRUDE and HARVEY leave.

Beat.

QUENTIN mounts his swing.

EDWARD: What are you doing? You hate that thing.

QUENTIN: The ground doesn't hold me anymore.

He swallows emotion.

So long, suckers.

QUENTIN's swing lifts him up through the hatch and off.

EDWARD is left alone on the stage.

Beat.

EDWARD opens the school rucksack and looks inside.

He smiles and pulls out a pair of jeans, a t-shirt, socks and trainers.

He puts them in a pile on the stage and stands up.

He looks at the audience uncertainly.

Beat.

He addresses them –

EDWARD: At the end of his trial Oscar Wilde asked to speak in the courtroom, but he was drowned out by the people in the gallery who were shouting, chanting one word – shame.

He begins to undress out of his Edward costume throughout the following –

I think the first part I ever played was myself. At school I studied how the other boys behaved and I copied them, I put what I saw into action – I changed the way I walked, the way I talked, the way I sat, the way I laughed. I suppose I'm still doing it. Dressing up. Still covering.

He goes to take off his undershirt, hesitates, then removes it. He is now stood in his underpants.

It's a sleight of hand – this covering up. An attempt to distract your eye from the other stuff. The stuff that I'm willing you not to see – the buckled king howling in his pit.

He dresses in the clothing that he retrieved from the rucksack throughout the following –

After his assassination, a funeral procession was held for Harvey Milk. People took to the streets and 40,000 candles were lit in his honour.

He is fully dressed now.

Shame wants us to feel like we're on our own, but we're not.

He begins relighting the candles around the space –

There's a bust of him, Harvey, in San Francisco. In City Hall where he worked, where he was murdered. It's only made of bronze or whatever, but there's a twinkle, somehow, in the eyes.

They've put him at the top of the stairs, on this landing, in this great grand entrance hall. He's a little tucked in the corner, but he's there. It's where couples get married now – right in front of him. This shiny bust, smiling, beaming at them as they say their vows. Men and women. Men and men. Women and women. Humans. Stating proudly who they are. Declaring love. With him twinkling behind them.

He finishes lighting the candles.

He steps forward, takes the audience in.

Beat.

It's all out there waiting for us. All of it. It's ours.

He takes a deep breath in and then exhales.

All the doors in the auditorium and on the stage open.

Beat.

He smiles broadly.

A high-octane, acoustic version of an eighties gay anthem is sung by the cast.

All the characters join EDWARD on stage for a triumphant jig.

QUENTIN appears through the hatch and swings above them, as they dance together joyfully.

End.